A TEACHER'S GUIDE TO
SPECIAL
EDUCATION

A TEACHER'S GUIDE TO SPECIAL EDUCATION

DAVID F. BATEMAN & JENIFER L. CLINE

ASCD | Alexandria, VA USA

 Council for Exceptional Children Arlington, VA USA
The voice and vision of special education

1703 N. Beauregard St. • Alexandria, VA 22311-1714 USA
Phone: 800-933-2723 or 703-578-9600 • Fax: 703-575-5400
Website: www.ascd.org • E-mail: member@ascd.org
Author guidelines: www.ascd.org/write

Deborah S. Delisle, *Executive Director;* Robert D. Clouse, *Managing Director, Digital Content & Publications;* Stefani Roth, *Publisher;* Genny Ostertag, *Director, Content Acquisitions;* Allison Scott, *Acquisitions Editor;* Julie Houtz, *Director, Book Editing & Production;* Katie Martin, *Editor;* Donald Ely, *Senior Graphic Designer;* Mike Kalyan, *Manager, Production Services;* Keith Demmons, *Production Designer*

Published simultaneously by ASCD, 1703 North Beauregard Street, Alexandria, Virginia 22311 and the Council for Exceptional Children, 2900 Crystal Drive, Suite 1000, Arlington, Virginia 22202-3557. CEC is a nonprofit, nonpartisan membership association for teachers of exceptional students from kindergarten through high school. Alexander T. Graham, Executive Director; Lorraine Sobson, Professional Publications.

All referenced trademarks are the property of their respective owners.

All web links in this book are correct as of the publication date below but may have become inactive or otherwise modified since that time. If you notice a deactivated or changed link, please e-mail books@ascd.org with the words "Link Update" in the subject line. In your message, please specify the web link, the book title, and the page number on which the link appears.

PAPERBACK ISBN: 978-1-4166-2201-7   ASCD product #116019   n6/16   CEC product #P6229
PDF E-BOOK ISBN: 978-1-4166-2203-1; see Books in Print for other formats.
Quantity discounts: 10–49, 10%; 50+, 15%; 1,000+, special discounts (e-mail programteam@ascd.org or call 800-933-2723, ext. 5773, or 703-575-5773). For desk copies, go to www.ascd.org/deskcopy.

Library of Congress Cataloging-in-Publication Data

Names: Bateman, David (David F.) author. | Cline, Jenifer L., author.
Title: A teacher's guide to special education / David F. Bateman, Jenifer L. Cline.
Description: Alexandria, Virginia : ASCD, 2016. | Includes bibliographical references and index.
Identifiers: LCCN 2016012633 (print) | LCCN 2016019776 (ebook) | ISBN 9781416622017 (pbk.) | ISBN 9781416622031 (PDF)
Subjects: LCSH: Special education–Study and teaching–United States. | Children with disabilities–Education–United States. | Special education teachers–United States
Classification: LCC LC3981 .B37 2016 (print) | LCC LC3981 (ebook) | DDC 371.9–dc23
LC record available at https://lccn.loc.gov/2016012633

25 24 23 22 21 20 19 18 17 16   2 3 4 5 6 7 8 9 10 11 12

A TEACHER'S GUIDE TO
SPECIAL EDUCATION

Introduction

With general education classroom teachers facing increased demands—from additional assessments to accountability to larger class sizes to working with students with disabilities—the profession of teaching is more complex and challenging than ever. We don't have all the answers for dealing with its every demand, but we do have concrete suggestions and descriptions of procedures and processes that can change the way teachers work with students with disabilities. Like other students, those with disabilities are expected to achieve in the general education classroom, and it is often the general education teacher who is responsible for that achievement.

This book is designed for you, the general education classroom teacher. Educating students with disabilities is most likely taking up more of your time each year. Parents and students look to you for information about learning strategies, standards, curriculum, accommodations, and modifications. There is a lot to know. Some of the issues related to students with disabilities are about paperwork and compliance, which may seem different from the content demands you face daily, but these elements are actually closely intertwined.

In this book, we address daily issues you are likely to encounter in working with students with disabilities, whether they have an individualized education program (IEP), have a 504 plan, or are not yet identified. We bring together information that will help you understand the process of how a student becomes eligible for special education services and your role in providing special education services and accommodations, and we present specific examples of what to do. We do not delve into the theory of the education of students with disabilities other than to confirm the belief in providing them with an education that improves their abilities and future possibilities. Federal law entitles them to such an education, and educational institutions are responsible for ensuring they receive it.

Our Purpose and What This Book Addresses

As a general classroom teacher, you will undoubtedly have students with disabilities in your classes. In fact, the majority of students diagnosed with disabilities spend most of their school time in the general education classroom (Friend & Bursuck, 2014). This was not always the case, and this shift has been happening continuously over the past 50 years. Furthermore, due to the provisions put in place to ensure equal opportunity for students with disabilities to access education and make progress in the curriculum, the situation is not going to change. Understanding the provisions and how to implement them is clearly important.

The realization that most students with disabilities spend the majority of their time in the general education setting steered the development of this book. Other factors guiding our efforts include the following:

• Students with disabilities are entitled to be included in general education classrooms to the maximum extent appropriate.

• The inclusion of students with disabilities is good for both students with and without disabilities.

• Parts (sometimes large parts) of a student's IEP are implemented in the general education setting.

• Students with disabilities have educational rights.

• Students with disabilities are children first and are not defined by their specific disability.

If you are like most general education teachers, it is likely you have received little if any training for working with students with disabilities. In this book we address this overarching problem by focusing on the following points: (1) your roles and responsibilities as the general education teacher, including working with other educators who are involved; (2) tools and information to assist with classroom instruction; (3) your relationship with parents of students with disabilities; (4) the range of students with disabilities, including those who do not receive any special education services; and (5) the importance of sound data management.

Roles and responsibilities

Like many general education teachers, although you probably received great training in how to teach content—reading, mathematics, science, social studies, essay writing, and so on—you need guidance on the roles and responsibilities related to working with students with disabilities. You are looking for assistance understanding many factors, including your role in the special education process, your role in an IEP meeting, who the various people are who work with students with disabilities, where (and when) to seek help, needs related to students with 504 plans, what information you need to provide for evaluation reports, what to do for classroom management, and how to handle grading for students who may not be working on the same level as other students.

Classroom instruction

We realize that most general education teachers never set out to be special education teachers. However, we also know that although many teachers came to the profession wanting to teach content (e.g., mathematics, literature, science), the vast majority did so because they wanted to teach *students*. When the students in your classroom include students with disabilities—as is almost always the case—meeting this goal can be a challenge. We are here to help. Our goal is to help improve the lives of students with disabilities and to give you background knowledge and tools to assist you in doing this.

The parent-teacher relationship

Many parents know the names of only three adults in their child's school: the principal, the bus driver, and their child's teacher. Those whose children are eligible for special education services may also know the name of the special education teacher, but their primary contact will be you. You need to be ready to address their concerns, participate with them in meetings, and then be willing and able to provide an education that is appropriate for their child.

The range of disabilities

Serving students with disabilities is part of every general education teacher's career from start to finish; new teachers should expect to have students with disabilities during their entire teaching career. Those students come in all shapes and sizes and with various kinds of challenges, including learning, intellectual, social and emotional, or physical disabilities. In addition, an increasing number of students with disabilities have Section 504 plans (the topic of Chapter 5) and receive no additional assistance from special education staff; they are, therefore, the sole responsibility of the general education program.

Data management

Good teaching is good teaching. However, using good practices for the data management that is required for students with disabilities can potentially enhance the educational experience for all students if you expand and use those practices for everyone. Good data management may also decrease the number of students being identified for services by better tracking of academic and behavior problems and the effectiveness of the interventions put in place to address these problems. At a minimum, the steps you take to document efforts to improve instruction for students with disabilities will likely improve the process and efforts directed toward all students.

Reasonable Expectations and Assumptions

Given all these factors, what can you, as a general education teacher, reasonably expect when working with students with disabilities? Here are some basic assumptions you should make:

You can expect to get assistance for a student who needs help. You are not in this alone. Others you can rely on to help provide support for students who are eligible for special education and related services include administrators, special education teachers, providers of related services, and outside agencies. Work with them, rely on them, and support one another. Remember you are an important player on the educational team of students with disabilities—particularly because you are most likely the first person who will detect a need for additional support for a student. If you do not make others aware of the need and work with them to provide the assistance required, the student may lose valuable educational opportunities. Such assistance may come in the form of an observation with recommendations, suggestions for classroom arrangement, suggestions for instruction, classroom support staff, or individualized instruction in an alternate setting. This support will not come unless you work with the administration and support staff to develop a program that is appropriate, based on the student's individual needs.

You can expect to be an active participant in a student's evaluation and plan development. You are the primary teacher of students, including those who are identified as eligible for special education and related services. Many of the other adults who will be part of the evaluation team will see the student only in isolated instances or for limited periods of time. After the evaluation is complete, the general education teacher is often the one who must continue to provide services (Mastropieri & Scruggs, 2013).

Speak up. Make sure you are heard. You will most likely know more about this student's educational needs and classroom performance than anyone else on the initial evaluation team. Make sure you help students (eligible or not) to get assistance that will help them make progress.

You can expect to access school district resources. Districts offer a wide range of services for students with disabilities, some of which may include services provided by paraprofessionals; tutors; specialized service providers such as speech language pathologists, occupational therapists, and physical therapists; or programs designed to meet specific behavioral or vocational needs of students. In addition, reading specialists, school counselors, and special education teachers can help analyze content and

> **What a General Education Teacher Can Expect When Working with Students with Disabilities**
>
> - To receive assistance for a student who needs help
> - To actively participate in a student's evaluation for special education services and special education plan development
> - To access school district resources
> - To work with and get support from knowledgeable special education professionals
> - To access a student's special education records and assessment information
> - To be heard

behavioral issues and develop adaptations to address them. It is important to be aware of the continuum of services your district provides so that you may advocate access for your students who require them.

You can expect to work with and get support from special education staff to understand what is important to know about a particular student with a disability and the effects of that disability on the child's education. As previously noted, most students with disabilities of various kinds—learning, intellectual, social and emotional, and physical—spend most of their school time in general education classrooms. As a general education classroom teacher, you recognize problems before anyone else and can provide important information about the student's performance compared to typically developing peers. It is important to be able to work with the special education staff to use this information to develop and implement appropriate services for students. This is also the case for students who are not eligible. Often, others can deliver individualized supports or additional information or strategies to supplement the general education program you provide to ensure that all students make progress.

You can expect to work with providers of related services. Students who are eligible for special education services may require additional assistance in the form of related services from other professionals in order to receive an appropriate education. The challenge is that many of these providers work with the student for only a limited amount of time each week. The rest of the time the student is in the general education classroom. It is important to understand the efforts and instruction being provided by the related service providers so you can reinforce skills while the student is in the classroom. Additionally, it is important to be able to report to the related service providers any updates and concerns about progress or lack of progress.

You can expect to have access to a child's special education records and assessment information. When a child becomes eligible for special education and related services, a fairly large report is developed, analyzing performance from a variety of perspectives. This is an important document for you as a general education teacher to be able to read and understand, so that you can be ready to implement its suggestions. Included in this paperwork will be the results of testing completed by either the district or independent evaluators, along with copies of the student's IEP (relevant parts should have already been provided to you). You will see a lot of important and private student information, and you will need to sign a sheet indicating that you accessed these records, which are kept locked up. Some of the information may be kept online and accessed with a password. It is imperative that you honor student and family confidentiality and talk only with the professionals who need to know information about this child in order to do their job.

You can expect to be heard! As you can see from this list of basic assumptions, the role and expectations of a general education teacher are to work with others in identifying problems, following up on concerns, actively participating in the development and implementation of a plan, and sometimes being the main point person representing the interests of students in your classes. To do all these things effectively, you need to be heard and respected as a viable team member providing services.

• • • • • • • •

Working with students with disabilities in a general education classroom can be difficult. However, a lot of supports are available to ensure that these students receive an appropriate education.

In this book, we offer information to help you meet the needs of students with disabilities in your classroom. Use it to learn the steps to take, when to document, and when to seek assistance. The appendixes provide helpful resources, including a list of common special education terms and acronyms, definitions of disability categories, information on "people-first" language, information on accommodations, and checklists for effective multidisciplinary team meetings.

We are certain that no matter where you teach, you will have students with disabilities in your classes. Our job is to help you succeed as you work to ensure they receive the education to which they are entitled.

1

Special Education and the Laws That Affect It

In this chapter we discuss the main laws affecting special education and how they apply to you as a general education teacher. The omnibus Individuals with Disabilities Education Act (IDEA) and the Family and Educational Rights and Privacy Act (FERPA) provide important guidelines and, although the Every Student Succeeds Act (ESSA) focuses on *all* students, it also has certain implications for students with disabilities.

To provide context, we explain what special education is—its characteristics, who receives it, its purpose and goal, why access to the general education classroom and curriculum is important, and who the various professionals are who work with students with disabilities. We also cover the rights and roles of parents of students with disabilities, again pointing out information that is important for you to know. (Keep in mind that some students with disabilities do not require special education services but may be affected by Section 504 of the Rehabilitation Act of 1973; basically, Section 504 is an anti-discrimination statute. For more about Section 504, see Chapter 5.)

Public Law 94-142

The Education for All Handicapped Children Act (PL 94-142), which is frequently referred to as PL 94-142, provides guidance to states, allowing students with disabilities to access public education and providing financial assistance to states as supplemental funding for special education and related services. Passed in 1975, PL 94-142 mandated that in order to receive federal funding for special education, states had to comply with the law (Yell, 2015).

The outcome of PL 94-142, now referred to as the Individuals with Disabilities Education Act, or IDEA (PL 108-446), is special education as we know it. Most recently reauthorized in 2004, it is the main law regarding educational services for students with disabilities, and its specific components are important to their education. Before 1975, only a few small districts provided education for students with disabilities in the United States. At that time it was legal to prevent students with disabilities from receiving an education. PL 94-142 changed everything for students with disabilities, and public education became education for all.

Eight Core Principles of Special Education

Special education law as it currently stands embodies eight core principles:

- Child find/zero reject
- Nondiscriminatory evaluation
- Individualized education program (IEP)
- Free appropriate public education (FAPE)
- Least restrictive environment (LRE)
- Related services
- Parent participation
- Confidentiality

Understanding these principles can help you understand how special education is meant to be provided for students with disabilities; they can guide you as you work to ensure that students make progress in the general curriculum.

Child find/zero reject

School districts are required by law to seek out and identify every eligible student with a disability living within their jurisdiction. Once identified, with parental permission, *all* students identified as having disability and requiring special education are to receive an education based on their individual needs. It is important to understand that this principle extends to students who may have committed a serious offense. Such students are still eligible for services.

Nondiscriminatory evaluation

Before students with disabilities are eligible for special education services, they must receive a nondiscriminatory evaluation, which is usually conducted by the school district. The evaluations must conform to the following guidelines:

- Tests must be administered in the student's native language.
- Tests must be appropriate for the student's age and suspected disability.
- More than one test must be used in determining the disability and need for services.
- Knowledgeable and appropriately trained individuals must administer the tests.
- All areas of suspected disability must be assessed.
- All decisions about eligibility for special education and related services must be made by a team, not a single individual.
- To be eligible for special education and related services, students must meet specific criteria; school districts serve students' educational needs under specified disability categories.

Individualized education program (IEP)

All students eligible for special education and related services receive an individualized education program, or IEP. The IEP is one of the most important educational documents for a student with a disability, and it should be viewed as a contract between the district and the student's parents. The IEP lists the educational and intervention services to be provided for the student, specifying the types and amount of such services. The IEP serves many purposes: instruction, communication, management, accountability, monitoring, and evaluation.

Free appropriate public education (FAPE)

All students in the United States have the right to receive an education, but students who are eligible for special education and related services are entitled to receive a free appropriate public education, or FAPE, which may look very different than what the general education student receives. FAPE is the heart of special education, and it includes several elements. First, the educational services provided to the student (assessment, instruction, special transportation if needed, other specialized services) are all provided at no cost to the family. Second, the education must be appropriate in that it allows the student to make progress in the general curriculum and is tailored and planned according to the student's individual needs. It is important to note that an "appropriate" education does not require the best possible services, but must ensure adequate progress in the general curriculum. Third, FAPE means that the public education entity is responsible for educating students within its boundaries. Some students may have such severe disabilities that they need to attend a school outside of the district. When a district determines it is unable to provide a free appropriate public education for a student, it is still responsible for covering the cost for the student to receive that education in a different setting.

Least restrictive environment (LRE)

"Least restrictive environment" is not only a special education term, but also a legal principle—and one of the most important points for general education teachers to know about because it determines where a student with a disability is to receive education services. LRE requires that students with disabilities be educated with their chronologically aged peers to the greatest extent possible, and that typically means in the general education classroom.

Under LRE, students with disabilities who are in general education classrooms are provided with supports and services that meet their needs as much as possible. Students with disabilities are to participate fully, both academically and socially. In addition, the general education teacher is expected to differentiate the methods used to provide services so all students benefit from instruction. Students with disabilities are to be educated in the general education classroom until all available methods to meet their needs in this environment are tried and deemed unsuccessful. A more restrictive setting should be considered only if every available method has been tried in the general education classroom and the needs of a student are still not met. It is important to note that the meaning of "restrictive" is open to interpretation and depends on the specific circumstances. For example, a paraprofessional interacting with a student one-on-one all day in a general education classroom could result in a more restrictive situation than the student would experience in a separate setting for instruction, due to possible social repercussions.

Related services

In addition to special education services, a student may require related services. Section 300.24(a) of IDEA defines "related services" as those that "are required to assist a child with a disability to benefit from special education." They include but are not limited to the following components: transportation, speech pathology, audiology, physical therapy, occupational therapy, therapeutic recreation, social work, medical services, counseling, and recreational services.

You may have students in your classroom who have articulation difficulties, are uncoordinated, have poor handwriting, or face other challenges, but will not be able to receive related services even though they might benefit from them. To be eligible for related services, students must first qualify for special education under one of the qualifying categories. Related services cannot be provided as standalone services (with the exception of speech language services). Thus an IEP cannot contain only related services. The purpose of a related service is to help a student with a disability benefit from the special education program.

Parent participation

Before a student receives special education and related services, the parents or guardians must sign on. They are equal participants in the process and must give permission for the evaluation, participate in the development of the IEP, and agree to any changes in either the program or placement. As a check on the system, parents have the right to request a due-process hearing. Finally, parents may have access to the student's records, including evaluation reports, IEPs, and disciplinary reports. (We discuss parents' roles and responsibilities in greater detail later in this chapter.)

Confidentiality

As a general education teacher, you will hear a lot of personal information about students, especially those with disabilities. Needless to say, confidentiality is very important. You should discuss information about a specific student only with others who need to know. For example, a 3rd grade teacher might talk with the special education teacher about problems in the classroom with a student who receives services from that teacher but should not discuss these problems with colleagues who are not part of the student's educational team. Additionally, there needs to be a log of all personnel who see a student's special education records.

The Broader Picture: What Is Special Education?

IDEA defines special education as "specially designed instruction, at no cost to the parents, to meet the unique needs of a student with a disability"(Sec. 300.39.a.1). But beyond the definition and the various components mandated by law, what exactly is special education? In a broad sense, special education encompasses the academic, physical, cognitive, and social-emotional instruction offered to students who have one or more disabilities. Due to a specific disability, some students' needs cannot be met within what might be called the "traditional" classroom environment. Special education programs and services adapt content and teaching methodology and deliver instruction to meet the needs of each student.

Special education has four main characteristics. First, it is *individualized*. For example, a student with a learning disability might need a smaller class size with individualized attention in reading; a student with a physical disability might need specialized equipment and possibly some technology modification; a student with an articulation disorder might need intensive instruction and modeling to improve her ability to communicate with others.

Second, students who receive special education services may receive *modifications* of teaching strategies or programs. Some students require extensive modifications due to the nature and severity of their disabilities, whereas others require only minimal changes.

Third, students who receive special education services are systematically *monitored*. Data support all phases of the special education process. Data are used to determine qualification for services and as the starting point for the development of the IEP, in terms of present levels of academic and functional performance, which includes all academic, behavioral, and social skills. Appropriate assessment at the start of the IEP process provides baseline data from which future progress can be measured. Progress toward goals can be measured by the student's performance in relation to individual short-term objectives or through other means, as determined by the IEP team. The IEP must also include a statement of how the student's progress toward goals and objectives will be measured. The data accumulated from these measurements are used to assess the student's progress.

Fourth, students who receive special education services also receive *related services* necessary to help ensure an appropriate education. As noted in the earlier discussion about the eight core principles of special education, these services are an important and beneficial component of many students' programs.

Who receives special education services?

Parents and other staff may come to you requesting an IEP for a student who has been diagnosed with a disability. However, it is important to understand that to be eligible for special education and have an IEP, a student must (1) meet the disability criteria outlined in federal and state law and (2) require individualized instruction (i.e., instruction that is not available to the general population of students). If these two criteria are not met, then a student does not qualify, even if that student has a disability.

Keep in mind that some students may be diagnosed with a disability and only require accommodations. Those students would not qualify for an IEP because requiring accommodations is not the same as requiring individualized instruction. However, they may qualify for a Section 504 plan (see Chapter 5 for more about Section 504 plans). Some parents and educators believe a diagnosis of a disability from a clinical psychologist or a physician automatically makes a student eligible for special education and related services. The student may have a disability but may not necessarily need specially designed instruction, and is therefore not eligible for special education. If a student receives a diagnosis of a disability from someone outside the school district, the district should consider this diagnosis and review the student's educational performance closely to determine if special education is necessary. The student may well be eligible, but that determination is made only after a comprehensive evaluation.

A comprehensive evaluation includes all of the existing data gathered about the student through the referral process and any additional assessments needed to determine eligibility for special education. As part of this information, the general education teacher provides an assessment of the student's progress in the general education classroom. Also, observations of the student take place—probably in the general education classroom. The purpose of this assessment is to help determine present level of performance, instructional strategies that are both effective and ineffective for the student, and any accommodations and modifications that may be needed.

Obviously, as the general education teacher, you have a significant role in the evaluation process. Each district will administer the assessments differently or use different assessments. It is important that you talk with the special education teacher, school psychologist, or administrator to determine your role and the tools that are used. The initial evaluation report is used to determine if a student qualifies and what special education and related services the student needs. And it is worth repeating that the determination that a student is eligible for special education and related services is a team decision, not a decision made by one person.

What is the purpose and goal of special education?

As noted earlier, students with disabilities have been historically excluded from education services, and by definition they need something different than what is provided for all students in order to be successful. The purpose of special education is no longer just to give these students access to education, but rather to teach the skills they need so they can be successful in the general education setting or develop as much independence as possible for adult life. Once students are receiving special education services, the goal is to enable them to use their potential to benefit from education and to build their skills to the point that the services are no longer required.

This goal is accomplished via individualized programs designed to address students' needs in accordance with IDEA, and it leads to increased responsibilities for general education teachers. In fact, only a small proportion of students with disabilities currently receive more than 60 percent of their education outside the general education classroom (U.S. Department of Education, 2013).

How much should a student benefit from special education?

Over the years, courts have attempted to help define how much benefit a student with a disability should receive from special education. Court cases regarding the implementation of IDEA have stated that IDEA does not require schools to provide students with the best or an optimal education, nor to ensure that students receive services to enable them to maximize their potential. Instead, schools are obligated to offer services that provide students with "some educational benefit" (*Board of Education of the Hendrick Hudson School District v. Rowley*, 1982). Courts sometimes refer to this as the "Cadillac versus Chevrolet" argument, with the student entitled to a serviceable Chevrolet, not a Cadillac (*Doe ex rel. Doe v. Bd. of Ed. of Tullahoma City Sch.*, 1993).

Some courts refined the "some educational benefit" standard to require that students achieve "meaningful benefit" or make "meaningful progress" in the areas where their disability affects their education. In *Rowley*

(1982), the Supreme Court of the United States mentioned that grades and advancement from grade to grade were factors in assessing benefit for mainstreamed students. Post-*Rowley*, courts have viewed passing grades and grade advancement as important factors in determining if students have received educational benefit. However, schools often modify grades for students with disabilities, so grades lose their validity as a measure of benefit or progress.

Some people may conclude that the lack of substantive standards for combined with the current "Cadillac versus Chevrolet" perspective changes expectations for students with disabilities compared with their typically learning peers. However, for many students, as long as the teacher knows what is in the IEP, and as long as the program is developed to appropriately meet the students' needs, the expectation of educational benefit is not lower for a student who receives special education services, it's just different.

Access to the General Education Classroom and Curriculum

There should be support for maintaining special education classrooms as part of the continuum of services. Some students require more assistance with academics and life skills, or their behaviors are such that they require a small classroom environment with more supports than can be provided in a general education classroom. However, there are a number of drawbacks associated with removing students with disabilities from general education classrooms, including the following:

• The general education classroom is where same-age peers are educated, and therefore it promotes social, emotional, and academic equality for all students.

• When appropriate support is provided, *all* students can benefit from inclusion. With so many diverse learners in today's general education classrooms, a general education teacher armed with better teaching tools will be better equipped to reach typically developing students as well (Friend & Bursuck, 2014).

• The removal of students from the general education classroom carries an associated stigma, including possible ridicule (Mastropieri & Scruggs, 2013).

• When students leave the general education classroom to receive support, they often lose valuable instructional time. For example, if students are "pulled out" for reading instruction when general education science content is being delivered, they may miss the opportunity to gain important science knowledge. Although the ideal is to remove students only from the classes that they are unlikely to benefit from, this is often not the case, due to scheduling conflicts.

Other researchers, such as Morse (1995), have discussed the disadvantage of students not receiving adequate services in a pullout program.

Educators and others have noted academic, social, and emotional pros and cons in both inclusive and special education settings for students with disabilities. But one viable alternative approach focuses on the restructuring of schools to allow for flexible learning environments with flexible instruction (Mastropieri & Scruggs, 2013). In a successful "merged" system, practices and methodologies are supported administratively and set high expectations for all students (Friend & Bursuck, 2014).

Who Are the Professionals in Special Education?

Providing services for students with disabilities is a team affair, and some students have many members on their team. Some of the following individuals provide direct support, whereas others play a more indirect role.

General education teachers are often the first persons to notice a student has a disability, can compare the student to others of the same chronological age and grade, and then are responsible for implementation of some services for the student. The general education teacher is the person on the team knowledgeable about curricular expectations and methods for differentiating so students with disabilities can make progress. Also, many parents will use the general education teacher as a point of contact for questions and concerns about educational services.

Special education teachers participate in meetings to help determine whether a student is eligible for services, and they are the professionals who are responsible for the facilitation and management of students' IEPs. They are often responsible for writing the goals and objectives of the IEP, and they work closely with the general education teacher on implementation of some of those goals and objectives. Sometimes they work directly with students to provide remedial or developmental instruction. Their specific role may vary dramatically depending on a student's individual program. Some special education teachers spend time in the general education classroom assisting the general education teacher and eligible students.

School administrators often provide indirect services for students with disabilities by ensuring proper implementation of policies, procedures, and

---

The Professionals Who Provide Special Education Services

- General education teachers
- Special education teachers
- School administrators
- School psychologists
- School counselors
- Speech language pathologists
- Occupational therapists
- Physical therapists
- Audiologists
- Paraprofessionals
- Clinical psychologists, behavioral specialists, and other outside professionals

---

financial responsibilities. School administrators range from building-level principals to districtwide administrators; all are important in working behind the scenes to make sure others can provide services.

School psychologists are licensed to administer assessments to help determine a student's eligibility for special education and related services. They often also provide consultation to classroom teachers for students who have problems with social and emotional issues.

School counselors are responsible for *all* the students in the school, so although they are not providers of specific special education services, they can be valuable resources for students with disabilities. For example, in some states they are responsible for developing students' Section 504 plans (see Chapter 5). They can also help students deal with social and emotional issues and provide resources for those students who need access to such basic provisions as clothing and food.

Speech language pathologists work with students who have issues related to communication. They assess, participate in meetings to determine eligibility, develop goals and objectives, and then work to provide instruction for students who may need assistance with a variety of issues, including articulation disorders, language issues, or physical problems with tongue movement or mouth and throat issues. The speech language pathologist may also be a resource in a student's development of social skills and the understanding and use of social communication.

Occupational therapists work with students who have problems with fine-motor control. Fine-motor control helps students with such things as grasping, writing, cutting, and using buttons, among other activities.

Physical therapists work with students who have difficulty with gross-motor activities. They often help students who have difficulty with muscle strength, balance, posture, and mobility. For students with more severe physical disabilities, they (along with other staff) also help with positioning, lifting, and transferring of students.

Audiologists help diagnose problems related to the ear and specifically to hearing. Often audiologists help determine if a student would benefit from a hearing aid or other amplification devices (personal or classroom).

Paraprofessionals work under the direction of a teacher or an administrator to provide direct services for students with disabilities. Paraprofessionals can have different titles, including classroom aide, teaching assistant, or one-on-one assistant, and they have widely different roles from class to class and building to building. One may provide reading assistance in a classroom, while another may help with positioning of a student with a physical disability, while yet another might help a student who has an emotional disorder deal with stressful situations.

Outside professionals are not employed directly by the district, but many states rely on them to help meet the needs of students with disabilities. Some of these professionals include clinical social workers and behavioral specialists.

The professionals highlighted in the preceding paragraphs typify those that you, as a general education teacher, are likely to see in your school. Others who also provide services typically work only with students who have a disability that is rare or more severe. Examples of others who might provide services include the following:

- Orientation and mobility specialist
- Art therapist
- Therapeutic recreation specialist
- Interpreter for the deaf
- Technology specialist
- Personal care attendant (PCA)

Parents' Roles and Rights

Earlier in this chapter we noted that parent participation is one of the core principles of special education, and as a general education teacher, it is important that you understand the roles and rights of parents of children with disabilities. IDEA outlines the rights of parents of students with disabilities. Those rights begin with the initial request for assessment and flow all the way to being expected to be an active participant in IEP discussions, as well as discussions regarding placement and transition services.

Figure 1.1 delineates the basic rights that parents have regarding the education of their child.

Parents as team members

As Figure 1.1 illustrates, parents are active team members in the identification, programming, and evaluation components of the education of a student with a disability. Parents of students with disabilities have more rights regarding education than parents of students without disabilities because students with disabilities are historically a protected class. They were for many years excluded from the educational process, and the additional rights provided to their parents serve as a check on the system to help ensure the district is meeting the students' needs.

Figure 1.1 / Parents' Rights Under IDEA

1. The right **to request testing**. Parents have the right to request that their child be tested and considered for special education.

2. The right **to give approval for testing**. When a school district would like to evaluate a student for special education, the process cannot move forward without the expressed written consent of the parents.

3. The right **to bring information to the evaluation and IEP teams for consideration**. Parents have the right to present any information they feel is pertinent to consideration for eligibility or development of their child's IEP. The team is obliged to consider this information.

4. The right **to request an independent educational evaluation (IEE)**. If the parents disagree with the evaluation completed by the school district, they can request an independent evaluation from a professional not affiliated with the district.

5. The right **to have IEE results considered**. Parents can ask that the results from the IEE be considered as part of their child's educational programming and placement.

6. The right **to request an evaluation in a native or preferred language**. Parents can request their child be tested in their native or preferred language and that the evaluation be conducted with the assistance of an interpreter or technology supports to accommodate physical disability.

7. The right **to be interviewed as a part of the assessment**. Parents have the right to have their ideas about their child's progress (or lack thereof) included in the evaluation report generated by the district.

8. The right **to be informed of their rights**. School districts are expected to routinely provide parents with copies of procedural safeguards to assist the parents in making an informed decision about their rights under IDEA.

9. The right **to be a team member for the evaluation**. Parents have the right to participate as team members when their child is being considered for eligibility for special education and related services.

10. The right **to be a part of the IEP team**. If a student is found eligible for special education, parents may be a part of the team determining programming and placement for the student.

11. The right **to bring others**. Parents have the right to bring others to an evaluation or IEP meeting who have knowledge about the student or the disability, including an outside specialist, an advocate, or an attorney.

12. The right **to incur no cost**. Special education and related services are to be provided to the student at no cost to the student's parents.

13. The right **to access due process/mediation**. Parents have the right to call for a due-process hearing or mediation if there is a dispute regarding the identification, education, or placement of the student with a disability.

14. The right **to file complaints with the state**. Parents can file a complaint against the district with the state education agency.

15. The right **to receive notifications in writing**. Parents must receive notifications in writing whenever the school district proposes a change in placement or is seeking to commence additional assessments to determine programming and eligibility.

16. The right **to receive regular reports**. Parents can expect to receive regular progress reports on their child at the same rate as parents of students without disabilities.

17. The right **to access records.** Parents can access their child's records and request a change if the records contain incorrect information.

18. The right **to request explanation of information**. Parents can request that the district explain reports, records, and documentation kept about their child.

19. The right **to obtain copies**. Parents can ask for and obtain copies of reports, records, and other documentation kept about their child. There may be documents that parents do not have a right to obtain. A building or district administrator can provide further clarification.

It is imperative that educators value the parental contribution—and remember that students spend the majority of their time *outside* of school. If students do not miss a single day of school (including full-day kindergarten), by the time they graduate from high school they will have spent only 10 percent of their life in school. The other 90 percent is the responsibility of the parents. Granted, some of that 90 percent is time that students are asleep (one would hope), but it is still the parents' responsibility to make sure their children are safe and provided for. It is the parents who help with sleeping problems, medical problems, finding help for services on weekends and summers, and countless other matters.

Although parents have an essential role as team members, it is important to acknowledge challenges that some teams face. Sometimes parents of children with disabilities view professionals as their "enemies"—as being difficult to work with and causing problems rather than providing help for the parent. According to Burke (2012), the biggest problems described by parents include teachers not understanding their child's disability, teachers not demonstrating commitment to the job, teachers not demonstrating respect to minority families, concern about the reception of services, too much jargon for the parent to understand, and disproportionate power in special education meetings. Burke (2012) states

> Regarding professional skills, for example, parents want school personnel to (1) understand the disability of their child and (2) learn about their child as an individual. School personnel need to recognize when they do not know something, admit that they do not know, and, subsequently, seek out the answer. For both general and special education teachers, it is important that teachers find information about the disability of the student and corresponding interventions. (p. 201)

It is important that as school districts work with parents to provide services for students with disabilities, the parents' rights and contributions are acknowledged and respected. Students will be best served when all members of their teams are functioning together.

To ensure that parents and educators have the knowledge and skills necessary to form effective teams on behalf of students with disabilities, districts can provide a number of supports (see Figure 1.2 for a list of the basics).

Figure 1.2 / Recommended District Supports for School Staff and Parents

- **Provide learning opportunities for educators to meet their basic obligations** to work effectively with families and for families to meet their basic parenting obligations.

- **Ensure systematic two-way communication** (school to home and home to school) about the school, school programs, and students' progress.

- **Provide learning opportunities for educators and families to work together** so that both can fulfill a wide range of support and resource roles for students and the school.

- **Provide educators and families with the skills to access community and support services** that strengthen school programs, family practices, and student learning and development.

- **Prepare educators and families to actively participate in school decision making** and exercise their leadership and advocacy skills.

- **Provide educators and families with strategies and techniques** for connecting learning at school with learning activities the student can do at home and in the community.

Parents and IEP approval

When parents make suggestions regarding the educational placement and programming for their child, they have a long-term interest in mind. Parents of some students with disabilities will be expected to help provide and care for their child for many years after high school.

Congress rightfully provided a check on the provision of care for students with disabilities by giving parents the right to approve the IEP. School districts cannot evaluate, place, or provide services for students with disabilities without parental consent. All states have detailed notices about procedural safeguards that are provided to parents to make sure they understand their rights, and one of the most important is IEP approval and consent.

When the terms "consent" or "parental consent" are used in IDEA, the meaning is the same as the meaning of the term "informed written consent." It means that the parent has been fully informed regarding the action for which parental consent is being requested.

Parents have the right to disagree with decisions that the school system makes with respect to their child with a disability. This includes the school's decisions about the following:

- The identification of the student as a "student with a disability"
- The student's evaluation
- The student's educational placement
- The special education and related services that the school provides to the student

What should parents do when they don't agree with the school system regarding any one of these matters? In such cases, it's important for both parties to first discuss their issues and try to reach a compromise or an agreement. The compromise can be temporary. It could be a trial agreement regarding transportation or the use of an aide in the classroom. The district should gather data to determine if the trial measure is working.

If a disagreement persists, the law and regulations include ways through which parents and schools can resolve disputes. These include the following mechanisms:

- *Mediation* brings the parent and a representative of the school together with an impartial third person to talk about the areas of disagreement, in an attempt to reach an agreement.
- *Resolution* begins when the school system receives a parent's due-process complaint and a meeting is held between parents and relevant members of the IEP team who have specific knowledge of the facts identified in the due-process complaint.
- *A hearing* occurs if the resolution discussion fails. The parents and the school present evidence before an impartial person (called a hearing officer), and that individual issues a decision that resolves the issue or issues.

Keeping parents informed

Keeping parents informed is one of the best suggestions we can offer to schools and districts, and as a general education teacher, you have a major role in this effort. Parents need to be kept informed about their child's progress, any problems that may occur with their child's education, and any plans for future services.

Remember that parents are an essential part of the student's team and their rights are embedded throughout the procedures of special education. Some would argue that the most important work you can do to help students with disabilities is to build a trusting working relationship with their families.

Withdrawal from special education programs

Along with the right to give consent for their child to participate in special education programs, parents have the right to revoke that consent at any time. They may do so even after a student has been placed into special education and things seem as though they are going well (Letter to Cox, 2009). This means a parent may remove a child from special education at any time.

> **What Parents Need to Know**
>
> - Grades, both good and bad
> - Behaviors, both good and bad
> - Problems with academics
> - Problems with peers and other social difficulties
> - Problems with transportation (such as on the bus to and from school)
> - Schedule changes
> - Any need for assistance

FERPA

The Family Educational Rights and Privacy Act (FERPA) of 1974 (PL 93-380) is a federal law protecting the privacy of student education records. FERPA gives parents certain rights with respect to their child's education records. These rights transfer to the student when he or she reaches the age of 18 or attends school beyond the high school level.

Here are the main points articulated in FERPA:

• Parents of students up to age 18 have the right to inspect and review the student's school records unless their rights have been terminated under state law.

• School district employees can also access a student's education records when doing so is necessary for their job.

• School districts are required to keep a record of all people, other than school district employees, who access a student's school records.

• Parents have the right to receive one free copy of their child's records.

• Parents may request in writing that the school district change the student's school records if they believe them to be inaccurate, misleading, or in violation of the privacy or other rights of the student.

• Once a student turns 18, parents have the right of access to their child's educational records only if they have the student's written consent, unless the parent maintains the student as a dependent for tax purposes or has retained custodial rights of the student.

ESSA and How It Relates to IDEA

IDEA and the Every Student Succeeds Act (ESSA) of 2015 (PL 114-95) are the two most important federal laws related to the education of students in the United States. As discussed earlier in this chapter, IDEA focuses on ensuring that students with disabilities are able to access appropriate education, which involves determining the individual needs of the student and building a program that addresses those needs. ESSA, on the other hand, focuses on improving the education of *all* students. Therefore, the provisions of ESSA also apply to students protected under IDEA.

When ESSA was signed into law in 2015, the goals it set provided both benefits and challenges for districts and students. Let's look briefly at the goals of ESSA and highlight their impact on special education services.

Develop challenging academic standards and benchmarks. This concept adheres to the intent of IDEA; however, when developing individual programs for students who have more severe disabilities, the inclusion of academic standards and benchmarks has been a bit of a challenge. Doing so is possible, however, and because of this goal, standards-based IEPs are being developed and implemented.

Develop annual academic assessments. This goal relates to measuring growth and determining if school programs are working for the majority of students. However, special education has included regular assessment of student progress since its inception. This part of ESSA implements a good practice that has been happening in special education for a long time.

Limit alternative tests. In the past, IEP teams could determine that students with disabilities did not need to take state and district assessments. Now the expectation is that all students will participate. However, alternate assessments for up to 1 percent of the population are available for students with disabilities who are unable to participate in the regular assessments.

ESSA and IDEA work together to ensure students with disabilities have the following:

• Performance assessment based on the same standards as their general-education peers
• Supports to help them succeed
• Assessments to help track their progress

Summary

This chapter discussed the law as it relates to students with disabilities. It also helped to define what special education is, who receives special education, and the purpose of special education; listed the professionals in special education; and covered in detail the rights of parents. Understanding IDEA and parent rights relating to special education is important to helping provide appropriate education for students with disabilities. As the general education teacher, you are an influential professional with an important responsibility to ensure that students with disabilities get the right services.

2

Educational Frameworks and the Pre-Referral Process

As a general education teacher, you have a wide range of learners in your classroom, and you are constantly responding to their individual needs. A number of educational frameworks are available to help you meet these needs, and an understanding of these frameworks and of various instructional strategies will provide you more options when working with the diverse learners in your class. You will also be gathering data and making observations to determine if what you are doing is allowing your students to move forward in the curriculum. In this chapter we discuss how the Response to Intervention/Multi-Tiered System of Support, differentiated instruction, and the Universal Design for Learning can help you fulfill these responsibilities. (For information about accommodations and modifications, which are important elements of instruction for some students with disabilities, see Chapter 4.) We conclude the chapter with information about the steps to take to refer a student for special education testing.

Response to Intervention and Multi-Tiered System of Support

Response to Intervention (RTI) is an instructional delivery framework with layers of preventative practices that teachers can use to target students' specific needs. The practices are "preventative" in that the goal is to ultimately prevent students from needing special education and related services. RTI is based on research stemming from the Institutes for Research on Learning Disabilities (IRLDs) from 1979 to 1983, and it became prominent when IDEA was reauthorized in 2004. The reauthorization included various changes and additions to the law, including the opportunity for states to permit the use of a process based on a child's response to scientific, research-based interventions when identifying students as having a specific learning disability. The framework has evolved since then to recognize that preventative interventions in academics and behavior are inextricably linked. The newly conceptualized model is referred to as Multi-Tiered System of Support (MTSS), which includes Schoolwide Positive Behavior Support (SWPBS) as well as RTI methodology for academic intervention. As a result, MTSS is now an umbrella term encompassing RTI. However, it is important to note that many educators use the terms interchangeably.

According to IDEA 2004, a student cannot be determined to have a disability if the determining factor is one of the following: (1) a lack of scientifically based instructional practices and programs in reading and math, or (2) limited English proficiency. Proponents of the RTI/MTSS model argue that the traditional "discrepancy" model, which assesses whether there is a significant discrepancy between a student's scores on a general "intelligence" test (such as an IQ test) and an academic achievement test, is problematic. First, they say, it is a "wait to fail" model, in which struggling students do not get intervention early enough because they are not performing significantly enough behind what is expected for their age or grade. They then fall further behind, and when tested later, they qualify because the discrepancy has grown. Second, opponents argue that the discrepancy approach does not provide the direct link to intervention necessary to help plan instruction. The RTI/MTSS model addresses both of these concerns.

The Critical Components of RTI/MTSS

- Universal screening of academic functioning
- A three-tiered intervention model
- Use of differentiated, research-based intervention strategies
- Continuous monitoring of students' performance

A three-tier framework

In the RTI/MTSS process, evaluation and intervention are essentially conducted concurrently. The model works to prevent failure by placing students in levels, or tiers, of instruction based on their individual needs (Kovaleski, VanDerHeyden, & Shapiro, 2013). Tier 1 involves screening and instruction that are available to all students—for example, an early literacy program is applied to all students and has both an instructional and a screening component. Students who are in a Tier 1 program are able to make progress and are performing at the expected level. Tier 2 typically involves assessing students' response to small-group instruction. Students receiving Tier 2 interventions are not performing at the desired level, but they are close to doing so and require some interventions to close the gap. Students receiving Tier 3 instruction typically have significant gaps in their learning that need to be addressed. Tier 3 involves intensive, more individualized intervention and then determining if the student needs special education and related services.

At each of these levels, teachers and others (reading specialists, for example) monitor and document student progress. Students in Tier 3 should be monitored more often than those in Tier 2, who, in turn, should be monitored more often than those in Tier 1, to determine not only student progress but also a need for more intensive support. The purpose of the interventions at all levels is to accelerate student learning and close the performance gaps so that the student is performing at the desired level.

Monitoring and gathering data

Response to Intervention and Multi-Tiered System of Support are a function of the general education program, which is largely responsible for the various processes and monitoring that are involved. Therefore, as a general education teacher, you play a significant role by gathering data and information that are considered when a team is determining if a student qualifies for special education services.

Some students respond well to the RTI/MTSS process and do not need a referral for special education. It is important, however, that you continue to gather data on the students' progress and confirm that the interventions are working. As noted earlier, the ultimate goal of RTI/MTSS is to prevent students from needing special education and related services. However, whether a student is determined eligible for special education or not, the collected data will help you make more-informed decisions about the educational needs of a student. Gathering and using data to make educational decisions for all students is simply good teaching practice.

Differentiated Instruction

Differentiated instruction is modified teaching that helps students with diverse academic needs and abilities to master academic content. You can differentiate instruction with an individual student, within a small group, or with a whole class. Differentiated instruction does not mean separate activities. The instructional activities should be related but changed to address the different ability levels of the students.

Here is a simplified, step-by-step description of how differentiated instruction works:

1. Start with the end in mind. What do you want all students to learn?
2. Determine how much the students already know about the topic.
3. Determine the students' skills and what supports they need.
4. Determine the students' interests and how you can use those interests to help anchor concepts.
5. Determine the students' strengths and build on those when covering concepts.
6. Determine time allocations to account for the needs of students who may require more time.
7. Prepare the learning environment and activities around the information you've gathered in the first six steps, and present the material.
8. Make note of what works with different students. Students may surprise you. You can use that information when planning for the next lesson.

Differentiated instruction enables you to challenge high-achieving students and to support struggling students; in essence, it allows you to provide for all students in your classroom. Teachers who use differentiated instruction match tasks, activities, and assessments with their students' interests, abilities, and learning preferences.

Four areas of differentiation

Sometimes people assume that differentiating instruction means giving certain students a different activity, book, or assignment instead of having them do the same or similar work as others in the classroom. Although some students who have disabilities will, in fact, require a replacement program, that situation is the exception. The important distinction between *differentiated* instruction and *different* instruction is that in the former, the same curriculum is addressed through the use of different supports and expectations for output, whereas the latter calls for a separate and different curriculum. Differentiated instruction targets and accommodates students' diverse needs and deficiencies in the learning process through careful changes in one or more of these four areas: content, process, product, and environment.

Content differentiation can be broadly defined as differentiation of what students need to learn and how they will access the information. Expectations related to learning the content correspond to the different levels of Bloom's taxonomy. For example, students who have no knowledge of the content may focus on remembering or understanding basic concepts, whereas students with greater prior knowledge may focus more on evaluating or creating something with the concepts. Here are some examples of differentiated content related to a reading assignment:

- Matching vocabulary with definitions
- Reading passages and answering questions
- Determining what is fact and what is opinion
- Providing evidence to support a viewpoint
- Creating a project by using and applying the learned concepts

Process differentiation recognizes that not all students have the same learning style or require the same amount of support, and so the instructional processes are modified accordingly. Instructional materials can be delivered in ways that will support various learning modalities, such as visual, auditory, verbal, and kinesthetic. Process differentiation may also take into account that some students will require one-on-one support from the teacher, some will work well when paired with a peer or in small groups, and others will be able to work alone. Here are some examples of process differentiation:

- Using textbooks or materials with a lot of visual elements
- Using audiobooks
- Having students complete interactive assignments online

• Using manipulatives
• Allowing for group work

Product differentiation acknowledges that although all students are working toward the same goal, based on their individual needs they should have access to different ways of demonstrating that they have learned the material. Here are some examples of product differentiation:

• Having students write a story, present a play, or give a presentation to the class
• Asking students to prepare an outline of what they worked on and present it to the class
• Assigning students to develop a website related to the learned material

Environmental differentiation involves changing the way the class-room looks and feels. You can create a flexible, safe, and supportive environment that provides optimal learning conditions for students both physically and psychologically by focusing on classroom layout, teaching style, and classroom management strategies. Environmental differentiation includes decisions on whether to place students in rows or groups, or where students can spend their "free" time. It asks you to consider these things as ways to help students participate more fully in the classroom experience, with a greater focus on instruction—keeping in mind that more student engagement also translates into fewer behavioral issues. Here are some examples of environmental differentiation:

• Using small discussion groups for reading assignments
• Allowing students to take more responsibility for their own learning by giving them options on how they learn the material
• Having pillows or beanbag chairs for students to use when reading or working on certain activities
• Allowing some students to move around more
• Providing lighting that focuses students' attention on a certain area

RTI/MTSS and differentiated instruction as complementary partners

Both RTI/MTSS and differentiated instruction emphasize explicit instruction provided by the teacher. These frameworks focus on providing instruction and activities that match the learning level and needs of each individual student. RTI/MTSS focuses on how a *student* responds to targeted interventions, and differentiated instruction focuses on how the *teacher* provides instruction and uses instructional strategies.

RTI/MTSS and differentiated instruction complement each other in many ways. Both include the following features:

- Student-centered instruction
- Frequent monitoring of student learning and behavior
- Data-collection mechanisms that support instructional planning
- Support for teachers to identify skill deficits and plan instruction accordingly
- Teacher analysis of the student for areas of strength and weakness and to determine if there are any physical issues
- Encouragement of best practices
- Emphasis on data-based decision making
- Promotion of awareness of students' varying needs, skills, and learning styles, and the need for instructional practice to address these differences

Universal Design for Learning

Universal Design for Learning (UDL) is a framework that strives to ensure that everyone has access to learning. It takes into account students' different needs and learning styles, and it provides curricula and activities that allow multiple ways for materials to be presented and for students to demonstrate their understanding.

The UDL framework came about as a result of the passage of the Americans with Disabilities Act (ADA) of 1990 (PL 101-336). The goal of ADA was to make public places more physically accessible, enabling everyone to use doors, water fountains, walkways, and entrances, for example (U.S. Equal Employment Opportunity Commission, 2009). Just as the goal of ADA was to make buildings physically accessible, the goal of UDL is to make learning accessible. UDL draws upon best practices in teaching to make the classroom more accessible for all types of learners, including those with disabilities (Rose, Meyer, Strangman, & Rappolt, 2002). It recognizes that students perceive information differently, for a host of reasons. They vary in the background and experiences they bring to the classroom. Some may have traveled widely and seen and done things others have not; some may have had little or no exposure to books, or they may have had differing amounts of oral-language experience at home. Among students with disabilities, some have sensory impairments involving vision or hearing, whereas others have learning disabilities. These students may all be sitting in the same class, but no one instructional strategy is going to work for all of them. See Figure 2.1 for examples of strategies based on UDL. For more information on UDL's guidelines for learning, see http://www.udlcenter.org/sites/udlcenter.org/files/updateguidelines.pdf.

Figure 2.1 / Examples of Instructional Practices Revised for UDL

When presenting materials . . .

- Change the size of text or images.
- Speak more loudly or increase the volume of auditory presentation devices.
- Increase the contrast between text or images and paper or background.
- Change layout or visual images.

When teaching main ideas . . .

- Use multiple examples and nonexamples.
- Use cues to prompt or draw attention.
- Reduce the amount of extraneous information or features.
- Highlight key elements of text.
- Use outlines to help students understand how information relates to other skills or tasks.

To boost memory or retention

- Use sticky notes and checklists for reminders.
- Teach mnemonic strategies.
- Provide templates for filling in information.
- Use scaffolding to build on prior knowledge.
- Use concept maps.

To set and uphold behavior expectations

- Have three to five overarching behavior expectations.
- Make sure that rules are
  - Agreed upon.
  - Defined for the specific setting and location.
  - Clearly communicated and understood by all.
  - Taught in different settings.
  - Posted.
  - Demonstrated by adults.

UDL and behavior

Methods that allow students to more actively participate and learn, like those encouraged by UDL, have the added benefit of dramatically helping with attention and behavior problems. Students' negative behaviors increase when they cannot access material, when information is presented in a manner unclear to them and they can no longer contribute to the class, or when they feel others are doing significantly better than they are.

When you think about behavior, it is important to consider three components: safety, predictability, and consistency. All students need to know they are coming to a safe, predictable place that maintains a certain level of consistency. This kind of environment allows them to focus on the tasks at hand, including learning and socialization. Part of your role as their teacher is to address any concerns they may have. You need to make sure that any threats or distractions are minimized or eliminated.

Teaching appropriate classroom behavior skills and expectations can help to create a safe, predictable, and consistent environment, and some would argue that doing so is as important as teaching academic content. The time you spend on the topic is well worth it. Without good classroom behavior, providing good instruction becomes very difficult. (See Chapter 7 for specifics about rules and rule enforcement.)

UDL at the elementary level

Your goal as a teacher is to help all students to understand the lesson you are presenting and produce outcomes that will help you to determine if learning is occurring. As we noted earlier, you will need to individualize lessons based on the needs of the students, but the following is a starting point for formatting an elementary-level lesson that incorporates the principles of UDL:

1. *Goal*—Determine the goal for the lesson. How does it relate to the state standards? What are students expected to know at the end of the lesson?

2. *KWL*—Use a KWL chart to determine what the students *K*now, what they *W*ant to learn, and (when you have completed the lesson) what they have *L*earned. Organize your lesson around these activities.

3. *Options*—Think about the different options for presentation. Consider how the students learn, and present the information in ways that are compatible with their learning styles. Consider visual and auditory methods. Break the lesson into component parts. Use small groups based on the students' strengths and needs. Provide time for independent practice.

4. *Wrap-up*—Finish the KWL chart by having students discuss what they have learned. Allow them to express any new knowledge they have gained.

5. *Evaluation*—Give students oral and written feedback as they complete the various tasks the lesson includes. Some students may need an additional learning activity to address concepts again. Base grades on multiple criteria: knowledge, skills, group work, and effort.

UDL at the secondary level

Secondary teachers face a formidable challenge, given the increasing number of curricular expectations they must deal with, as well as the increasing diversity of their students. This situation makes it all the more important that teachers vary their instructional format to address the needs of all students—those with and without disabilities, and across all levels of achievement. Modifying instruction takes time, energy, and concerted planning, and the UDL framework can help with the effort. The framework benefits all students, not just those with disabilities, ensuring that all students have an opportunity to learn and multiple ways of demonstrating their understanding.

Here is an example of how you might apply the UDL framework at the secondary level:

1. *Pre-assessment*—Show a multimedia presentation on the topic to be addressed, and then talk with students about how the content relates to their lives.

2. *Background information*—Based on what you have determined from the pre-assessment, you may conclude that not all students will need to complete this step. But some students will need different methods and opportunities to tell you about or to demonstrate what they know.

3. *Project*—Divide students into groups, carefully considering their diverse needs, and assign all students a specific role.

4. *Presentation*—Have the members of the group present back to the larger group on what they have learned, with each playing a role in the presentation. As part of their presentation, have students develop an activity that will help the others understand the concept.

5. *Post-assessment*—Provide students with a rubric, along with a written assessment to determine what they have learned from the assignment. Also consider oral-based assessments for students with reading and written language difficulties.

6. *Evaluation*—Give students oral and written feedback on their completion of the various tasks. You may have to provide some students with another learning activity to address important concepts again. Base grades on multiple criteria: knowledge, skills, group work, and effort.

The Pre-Referral Process

The vast majority of students who receive special education services are found to be eligible after they start school. (A small number are identified as eligible before entering kindergarten, and they may access services from age 3 until they begin school.) For many children, the first days of school represent the first time they are being compared to other children and are asked to perform academic tasks. It is usually the general education classroom teacher who at some point notices differences among students in writing, reading, math, social skills, speech, or independent functioning. This is one of the most important things that can happen for a student—a professional's initial realization that the student may need to receive more assistance than other students require.

What is known as the "pre-referral process" begins when the general education program embarks on interventions and data gathering to determine if a disability is present. The school district must complete these steps before referring a student for special education services. Through this process you will gather valuable information that will be essential in determining next steps in the student's educational path, whether special education is part of the plan or not. Determining whether a student should be referred for special education services may require that you try various strategies and interventions multiple times, but ultimately you will have a better idea of what works for the student.

Your school will have a team to assist you with the pre-referral process. Make sure you know how to access this team for help and support. Some of the terms that are used for this pre-referral team include student assistance teams, teacher assistance teams, or preferred intervention teams; some districts use the RTI/MTSS process and team for pre-referral. Teams may have formal, regularly scheduled meetings, or the school may have someone who is the point person to go to when there is a need. In some schools, the principal or assistant principal is also involved to provide support in potential areas of need.

Steps to Take When Working with a Struggling Student

What are some of the characteristics of a struggling student? What are some questions you need to address to help make sure the student is making progress? Many of the determining factors as to whether a student is functioning satisfactorily in a classroom or needs to be referred for special education testing come down to data you gather as a general education teacher.

You can tap a number of sources for information and support to help you work to meet the needs of a struggling student. We recommend following a step-by step process, which we will detail in the section that follows.

Define the specific concern. What is it about the student's learning that causes you to be concerned? Be specific in your definition of the concern. Clearly define what behaviors are getting in the way of the student's learning (e.g., the student talks out, the student walks around the room at inappropriate times, the student does not follow the classroom rules). Analyze closely whether this is a problem because the student is unable to learn the material or because the student needs something different than what you typically provide. As a general education teacher, you may need to change how you provide instruction to meet a student's needs. Once you have clearly defined your concern, it will be easier to develop interventions, modifications, or instructional strategies to address the concern.

Gather data. Data are very important and will be used to determine how the student performs compared with others in the class, to determine if interventions or strategies tried are effective, and to track progress or lack thereof. To fully understand how the intervention or strategy is working with one student, you need to know the progress and performance of the student's peers. For example, if you gather data on a student you think is having problems and find out over a half-hour that the student is on task only 55 percent of the time, this indicates he is off task 45 percent of the time. That seems like a lot of off-task behavior, but it does not really indicate whether there is a problem. If everyone else (or at least a few representative others) is also on task only 55 percent of the time, then this student is functioning at about the same level as others, and the behavior is not indicative of a problem that is outside the norm. Provide some quantification of the extent of the problem. However, do not compare the student who you think has problems with your top-performing student.

Review the student's file. The file may include information about grades rising and falling during the year, attendance, medical or health issues, medications, or other educational interventions that have been tried or plans put in place. Learn as much as you can about the student's previous history. You will want to look for patterns that might help you understand what is happening with the student.

Talk with the student's previous teachers. Although talking with a student's previous teachers is not always possible, if it is, seize the opportunity. Last year's teacher may be able to give you information that could help you figure out the problem this student demonstrates, or at least give you advice about actions taken that worked and did not work. The teacher can also give you information about the student's earlier classroom interactions, which you can compare to what you are seeing. Don't be afraid to contact the teacher even if the student came from another school. This information is valuable and well worth the time and effort it takes to connect with that teacher.

Talk with the student. You might be surprised to find out what the student perceives the problem to be (if the student even perceives a problem). Students are often able to shed some light on what makes it easier or more difficult for them to learn. Maybe they are distracted by hallway noise or another student, or they cannot hear over the heating unit in the classroom. Some students may not be able to articulate the specific problem; with these students, it can be helpful to begin with open-ended questions that allow them to describe what they are experiencing and provide you with direction for clarifying follow-up questions.

Compile samples of student work demonstrating the area of concern. It is important to have documentation so that you can show others the extent of your concern, with relevant examples. Is the student able to demonstrate math facts on one day but not another? Does the student consistently get poor grades, no matter what the assignment is? Are there distractibility issues causing the student to get good grades in a favorite class (PE, for example) and poor grades in reading and math? You need to define how the problem is affecting the student's learning or that of others. These work samples may also provide some insight into the degree of the concern as you begin to seek assistance and guidance from others.

Talk with the student's parents. Parents are a valuable source of information about their child's personality, interests, strengths, and needs. Make sure the parents know the status of their child's performance, what the specific concerns are, and what you could reasonably expect a student to be doing at this time. Be specific and honest, but also let the parents know that the student may be tested for special education and that you are doing everything possible to help at this point. Keeping parents informed about the progress of their child is an important task for all teachers. It is especially important if there are concerns. You do not want the parents to first hear about a concern when the district is recommending evaluation for special education. As the general education teacher, it is your responsibility to keep parents informed of their child's academic status as well as any interventions and strategies being implemented to help get the student back on track. Most parents will want to be part of this process and will be very helpful.

Involving the parents and seeking their assistance is also important for understanding the whole student. Maybe something is going on at home or after school that is having a significant impact on the student. Also, keep in mind that many parents, if able, will assist with additional instruction at home. Parents are your allies and an important support for the student. For example, they could potentially help monitor to make sure that homework is done and prescription medicine is taken, provide information about medical concerns, or share that the student is reporting being bullied on social media.

Talk with the principal. Principals need to know if there are any potential academic, behavioral, or social problems in the building. They need to know details, specific information about attempts made to help the student, and how this student relates to the functioning level of the other students in the classroom. Principals often serve on the multidisciplinary team that helps determine a student's eligibility, and they need to be kept informed so they can help plan assistance for the student, respond to calls from the parents for information, and help with future planning for staffing and budgeting.

Seek assistance from other staff and the school's intervention team. If your school is using a formal pre-referral or intervention team, those team members can also recommend interventions and generate ideas for things to try before the actual special education assessments begin. Some schools have clear, formal steps for the pre-referral team and process, whereas for others the procedure may involve no more than asking the teacher from down the hall for guidance. Find out from your principal what the process is for your building.

Implement multiple interventions. Based on what you know from the data you are gathering, you will need to attempt other interventions. Keep in mind that before making a referral for special education, you should have implemented at least three different interventions and have the data documenting the results of the interventions.

Implementing interventions and seeking assistance are often combined. You may be able to access other professionals in the building to provide some interventions or to give you guidance on interventions to implement. These professionals may include a special education teacher, a reading specialist, a behavior specialist, an administrator, or a speech language pathologist. Show them your data and seek guidance and suggestions about what to do.

The purpose of seeking advice from others about possible interventions is to help the student, and if possible, to prevent the need for special education. Often those who provide advice will ask you for an update in a few weeks to determine if the problems have improved or at least stabilized. Depending on the concern, you may want to provide an update sooner rather than later. For example, if the student is causing problems for others and preventing them from learning, then you would want a quicker fix to avoid additional issues. If the student is having problems with math facts, a longer report period may be necessary to allow the student adequate time to acquire the new skills.

Continue to document the results of interventions, strategies, and student progress. Some students will respond easily and rapidly to interventions, but others will not. You will need to try multiple interventions before the special education testing can begin. It is very important to ensure that you have implemented each intervention for an adequate amount of time to determine its effectiveness. This can be difficult when you are hoping to see changes quickly. If as a general education teacher you do not believe the suggested intervention will do any good or will compromise the effectiveness of another program or intervention, you need to speak up and discuss this with the team. Realize that many students have multiple issues they are dealing with that affect their education, and one intervention may not get to the root of the problem.

Share results of data from interventions with other team members. It is important to have data that reflect the intervention's effect on the student's performance. The data will help the team in determining whether a student needs additional assistance; if so, what kind; and if a referral for special education testing is warranted.

Maybe the suggested intervention worked wonderfully, or maybe the student made some progress with this intervention but not enough to reach the desired level of success. The team needs to be aware of issues the student is dealing with, any attempts you have made to make progress, and what has worked and what hasn't worked with the student. The team can make additional recommendations, help with data collection, and make sure that the results of what has been attempted are kept for future reference.

Once all possible general education interventions have been exhausted, the team may recommend formal testing for special education. The data you have about the student and the progress made (or lack thereof) compared with other students will be an important part of the referral for testing. Additionally, if you have kept the parents informed about a potential problem, it will be easier to get their understanding and permission for the testing process.

Summary

Various educational frameworks and strategies are available to general education teachers who have diverse learners in their classrooms, including students with disabilities. Frameworks such as Response to Intervention and Multi-Tiered System of Support (RTI/MTSS) includes a three-tiered intervention model and use of differentiated, research-based strategies. Broadly speaking, differentiated instruction involves making adjustments in one or more of four areas: content, process, product, and environment. Both RTI/MTSS and differentiated instruction seek to address the learning needs and levels of every student. Another educational framework, Universal Design for Learning (UDL), which emerged as a result of the ADA, strives to ensure that everyone has access to learning.

The general education teacher is often the first person to notice that a student may be having difficulty keeping up with other students in the class. This realization triggers the pre-referral process. The pre-referral process is designed to prevent students from requiring special education testing in the first place. The process consists of a series of steps to help determine whether a student really has academic, behavior, or social issues that are significantly different from those of the other students in the general education classroom and whether they warrant consideration for an individualized education program. These steps are important for helping everyone—administrators, other teachers, special education staff, and parents—to understand the specifics of the concerns. Each step may be repeated as often as necessary as you and the pre-referral team attempt to improve the student's learning. For example, you may have to redefine the problem as the student evolves in your classroom, and you will be asked to try multiple interventions before a referral for special education. These multiple interventions and the results of each are the baseline data used to determine appropriate assessments if a referral for special education is made.

If after completing the steps outlined in this chapter you continue to be concerned with the student's lack of progress, you may need to move toward a referral for special education to determine if the student has a disability. The referral and IEP processes involve many steps, most of which are intended to ensure that we are not taking students out of the general education classroom when, with changes, their needs could be met in that setting, and that they truly require special education services in order to move forward in their education.

3

The Referral and Evaluation Process

In Chapter 2 we described various educational frameworks and processes designed to support student success in a general education setting. However, some students will not respond to the different instructional strategies, modifications, and interventions you try. At this point, you need more, and more specific, information. Does this student have a disability that is interfering with educational progress? Does this student require an individualized educational program? A referral for special education is now appropriate.

In this chapter we detail the steps to take to refer a student, discuss the process of how students become eligible for special education and related services, and highlight your role as the general education teacher. We also provide guidance in regard to what general education teachers can learn from the assessments and apply to classroom instruction and strategies. We conclude with a discussion of parents' rights within the evaluation process.

Referring a Student for Testing for Special Education

If your attempts in the classroom and through the pre-referral process have not resulted in a change, and you think a student may have an underlying disability that is interfering with educational progress, the next step is to refer the student for testing to determine eligibility for special education and related services.

Once the referral is accepted, the multidisciplinary team outlined in IDEA takes responsibility. The members of this team may vary depending on individual state requirements and the area of the student's suspected disability. However, as we noted in Chapter 1, teams typically consist of an administrator, a special education teacher, a general education teacher (typically the classroom teacher), a parent or parents, and a school psychologist. The decision as to whether a student needs to be tested for special education is a school district responsibility, and the parents must be informed of the decision and the reason for it. The parents need information about the testing process and procedures, as well as their rights, and they need to give permission for the testing. The parents are a part of the assessment team and often are asked to complete questionnaires or contribute information they have on their child.

In your role as the general education classroom teacher, you will be the person who initiates most referrals for determination of eligibility for special education services. However, such referrals also may be initiated by the following other individuals:

• Other school personnel (including special education teachers, counselors, administrators, etc.)

• The student's parent or legal guardian

• Any other person involved in the education or care of the student

Requirements of a referral

Obviously, the work done in the pre-referral process, described in Chapter 2, will be helpful at this stage because it will help to document your concerns. When you request to have a student evaluated, be sure to include specific information as to why you think the student may need special education services and all of the areas of concern. It may be beneficial for you to work with the special education teacher or school psychologist when completing this paperwork. If you think, for example, that your student has difficulty in reading and has emotional

IMPORTANT POINTS

• The general education teacher is often the first professional to notice that a student needs assistance.

• The general education teacher plays a vital role in determining that a student is eligible for special education services.

• The process for determining eligibility may seem long, but a lot of work must be done to make sure a student really is eligible for special education and related services and to gather enough data to develop an appropriate plan for the student.

• Not all students who need assistance are eligible for special education services.

• Parental and student rights are a protected and important part of the referral process.

problems that need to be addressed, then ask that both areas be evaluated. It is also helpful to provide examples of the types of situations that appear challenging to the student. If you have them, provide any documents that indicate the student may have an impairment, such as letters from doctors or mental health providers. The following types of documentation can be very helpful.

Examples of the student's work. Depending on the problem area, furnish examples that are representative of the student's work. If a student has problems in multiple areas, you need to provide work samples for each area.

Examples showing how the student's work compares with the work of others in the class. Representative examples of the student's work and that of other students in the same class will enable you to accurately describe the student's functioning level. This comparison helps the multidisciplinary team determine the extent of the students' problems.

A list of intervention efforts and methods. List the different methods you have attempted or interventions you have used in efforts to improve the student's performance.

A list of materials used. Be able to describe the different materials you have used with the student. If the student is having problems with the reading books used in the classroom, try a different reading series and describe any differences in the student's experience. If the student is having problems with the tests from the textbook, describe how you have adapted them.

Data on the results of the interventions. The multidisciplinary team members need to see evidence and data on the success—or lack thereof—of the various methods you have used in your attempts to improve the student's performance. Many students' problems are complicated, and one week of a simple intervention may not do the trick. The multidisciplinary team will need to see what you tried and the associated data on the student's performance.

Your role in the referral process

Given that the general education classroom teacher refers most students who are tested for special education and related services, your role is incredibly important. As we've stated before, you often know the student better than anyone else in the building and understand the frustrations the student exhibits when faced with difficult material or the need to deal with certain social situations. If the student is found eligible for special education, you will most likely remain the student's main teacher. Therefore, you will need to continue to be an advocate for the student, follow up on the referral, provide needed work samples and classroom data, and be ready and able to explain to the student why he may be pulled out for testing. Finally, it is also important that you be available to answer questions from the parents about the process. If you do not know the specifics about the process, learn from the special education staff and make sure the parents' questions are addressed in a timely fashion. The parents will rely on you.

What happens once a referral is made?

Once the student has been referred for special education, you will be working with the multidisciplinary team. How the team is defined can differ from state to state; you can learn from the special education staff who makes up this team in your building. In some districts, the team members will be the same as those on the pre-referral team, and the difference will simply be in the assessments being given and the possible outcome of the testing. The most important point is that no students receive special education and related services unless they go through the referral and evaluation process.

It is important to know that the rights of the student and the parents change once a referral for special education has been accepted and testing begins. During the entire testing process, the student is considered eligible and has all the rights and protections of a student with a disability. These rights and protections continue until the student is determined *not* to be eligible.

After a referral for special education is accepted, the special education staff reviews the information and makes assignments to ensure that the following steps are completed promptly: (1) determine the necessary assessments; (2) obtain parents' written consent; and (3) complete the necessary assessments within a specified time line. Let's look at each of these more closely.

Step 1: Determine the necessary assessments. Based on the information provided by the referral, the special education staff determines the specific assessments that will be used to facilitate the determination of eligibility. If the student has a reading problem, the focus will be reading assessments; if the student has a problem with social skills, the focus will be social skill assessments; and so on. The information you provide as the general education classroom teacher is very important in determining the assessments. It is important to remember that the difficulty the student is having must be adversely affecting the student's education, which is one reason why the pre-referral data are so vital.

The Multidisciplinary Team

A multidisciplinary team consisting of individuals with different kinds of expertise will conduct the evaluation. The team generally includes the following:

- A *school psychologist or educational diagnostician* qualified to conduct and interpret educational assessments, including those for intelligence (IQ), achievement, behavior, and so on.
- *Special education teachers* qualified to conduct achievement and behavior evaluations and to make observations.
- *General education teachers* to provide documentation of the problems of the specific student and data on interventions and classroom performance.
- *Parents or guardians* to provide valuable insight into the student's behavior and personality in other environments.
- *Related-service providers* (physical therapist, occupational therapist, speech language pathologist, etc.) who are specialists equipped to provide information pertaining to specific areas of concern.

Step 2: Obtain parents' written consent. Students cannot be assessed for eligibility for special education without the expressed written consent of the parents. Different states use different terms for this step, but a document will be generated for the parents to sign listing the specific area or areas of concern and, broadly, the assessments that will be used to determine the student's eligibility. The permission to evaluate (terms will vary from state to state) will be provided to the parents. At the same time, the parents will receive a copy of their procedural safeguards (a detailed listing of their rights is summarized in Chapter 1). The district will not be able to start the testing process until it receives written parental consent.

Step 3: Complete the necessary assessments within a specified time line. Once the district receives consent, it must complete the assessments within specific timelines outlined in IDEA. As noted in Step 2, the district cannot start the testing process without the parents' consent, and it sometimes takes a week or more for the parents to return the form. However, once the form is returned, the district has, at most, 60 school days to complete the evaluation (some states use 60 calendar days). Ask a special education administrator for the specific number of days for your state.

The evaluation must be comprehensive and use assessment tools and strategies that are technically sound and accepted. Most students receive a battery of formal assessments measuring intelligence, achievement, behavior, disability-specific issues, hearing, and vision.

Informal observations and documentation of the student's past and current work will also be used for determining eligibility. Assessments may not be biased in regard to race, culture, language, or disability. The materials and procedures must be administered in the language and form most likely to provide accurate information.

The Evaluation Process

As noted earlier, once the student's parents consent to the evaluation, the school district has 60 school (or calendar) days to complete the assessments. During this time, the student continues to receive instruction through the general education program, and it is important that you continue to collect data on the student's progress and implement any strategies that help. As the assessment information is being gathered, the student may be pulled out of your classroom multiple times for testing from various individuals. In addition to the school-based assessments, reports and information from outside agencies may be gathered for consideration. A team meeting will be held at which all the assessment results are reviewed and considered to determine eligibility.

The parents and the student may have questions during this part of the process. Again, it is very important to be able to answer their questions and address any concerns, and to make sure other members of the multidisciplinary team are aware of the concerns. Questions or concerns about the evaluation process could range from "How long does it take?" to "What should we expect from the school psychologist?" to "Does this mean my child has to go into special education?" Take the concerns and questions seriously. Some parents are afraid that giving consent to testing means their child will be enrolled in special education classes. It is always important to explain each step of the process to the parents, along with their rights. Parents need to understand that they can choose to *not* have their child participate in special education programs even if the student qualifies for services.

Because the student is going to be pulled out of the classroom for testing, you will have to make sure the student gets assistance with making up the work missed. This will require planning on your part, since in many cases the student already has been determined to be behind (on some measures), and pulling her out of instruction could potentially cause her to fall further behind. You will also need to work with the individuals who will be pulling the student out for testing to find times that work best, so the student won't, for example, be missing the party at the end of the week or a favorite weekly activity. You don't want the student to be thinking about the fun she is missing while she has to answer reading and math questions.

Most likely several people will be coming to your classroom to observe the student. Inform them about your schedule and the activities you are doing with the student, and work with them to determine the best times for their observations. Also, make sure the observer knows when the student might not be in your classroom. For example, the student may be pulled out for additional reading assistance, or may be being assessed by the school psychologist, or there may be a field trip. Keep the observers informed about this and any changes to the schedule.

Ideally, if the student has a problem in reading, the observer would come during the class time devoted to reading. Make sure the observer knows who the student is and has a place to sit that is comfortable but not intrusive to the rest of the class. If the other students ask whom the person is observing in the classroom, shift their attention and say the observer is there to observe you (which is partly true).

Keep in mind that while the process for determining eligibility is moving forward and individuals are coming to the classroom, the student is still your responsibility. It is important that you continue to try new interventions to improve the student's performance. Additionally, keep gathering data. The 60-day evaluation period is a long time (it may be shorter than that, but no longer), and you may notice changes in the student's performance during that time. Be ready and able to bring the latest data to the meeting where team members will discuss the evaluation results. The latest information will be very important for the others to hear.

Your Assessment of the Student

You may be asked to provide a write-up of your views about how the student is doing in your classroom, which is referred to as a classroom-based assessment. At other times you will be required to complete forms that request information to be included in the final evaluation report and used to help determine eligibility. The components you contribute about the student should include the following:

- A statement about any forms completed
- The date the information was provided for the report
- A list of the student's strengths

• A list of concerns you have as the student's general education classroom teacher

• A statement of how the student compares with the average students in the classroom

• A statement describing anything out of the ordinary regarding this student's class schedule or day

• Any accommodations or modifications used that are helpful to the student

• List of current grades

Figure 3.1 shows a classroom-based assessment for an elementary student, and Figure 3.2 (see pp. 53–55) shows an example of a classroom-based assessment for a secondary student. Remember that the purpose of what you write is to help provide an accurate description of the student from your perspective so others can make an informed decision about the student's performance and whether the student might need special education.

Figure 3.1 / Sample Classroom-Based Assessment for an Elementary Student

Grade: 4

Teacher: Mrs. Claudette Berman

Date: September 24, 2016

Student's name: Griffin

What are the student's strengths?

- Positive self-image

- Always participates in class

- Will ask questions when he is unsure

- Exhibits friendly behaviors

What are your areas of greatest concern?

- Not always focused while working independently

- At least one grade level below in reading

continued

Figure 3.1 / Sample Classroom–Based Assessment for an Elementary Student (continued)

- Difficulty understanding and solving math facts and concepts

- Difficulty following written and oral directions (i.e., does better in a one-on-one situation where steps and procedures and directions can be explained multiple times).

How does this student compare with the average students (same-age peers) in your classroom?

- Average in work completion, overall behavior, behavior in halls, and aggression

- Above average with behavior in structured groups

- Below average in reading, math, spelling, writing, work accuracy, following directions, and behavior in unstructured groups

Grades: Failing in all academic areas

Factors affecting class schedule or day: Receives ESL (English as a second language) instruction during math and for a limited amount of time in language arts.

Accommodations or modifications that are helpful to the student: Benefits from his tests and assignments being read aloud as well as being given extra time to complete assignments and tests.

Determining Eligibility

Each state outlines the disability categories in which a student can qualify for special education services, and state law specifies the criteria that must be met for a student to be qualified under each category. Specific assessments may be required, depending on the disability category. However, regardless of the category, a classroom-based assessment and observation are required. The data and other information you provide as a general education teacher make up part (if not all) of the classroom-based assessment. If your state allows the use of RTI/MTSS to qualify a student who has a learning disability, those criteria for eligibility will also be outlined. To be declared eligible for special education and related services, the student must meet the criteria under one of the disability categories *and* demonstrate a need for individualized instruction.

Who makes the decision?

The determination that a child who is suspected of having a learning disability actually must be made by the student's parents and a team of qualified professionals, which must include the student's general classroom teacher

Figure 3.2 / Sample Classroom-Based Assessment for a Secondary Student

Teacher	Subject	Period	Completion of Class Curriculum	Class Participation	Behavior Control
JR	WORLD HISTORY	3	Below Average	Average	Average
	Attendance	**Motivation**	**Interactions with Adults**	**Interactions with Peers**	**Current Grade**
	Below Average	Below Average	Average	Below Average	D+

Accommodations used/needed in the general education classroom: Modified assignments, alternative assignments, additional time for assignments, additional time on tests, copies of notes, preferential seating, materials/tests read aloud, consultation with special educator

Comments: R started the quarter missing a lot of class. Lately he has been attending class and has had a great attitude. Hopefully, over time we can figure out a great system for my class that works well for him.

Teacher	Subject	Period	Completion of Class Curriculum	Class Participation	Behavior Control
MF	BASIC ENGLISH	1	Average	Above Average	Below Average
	Attendance	**Motivation**	**Interactions with Adults**	**Interactions with Peers**	**Current Grade**
	Average	Below Average	Average	Below Average	C

Accommodations used/needed in the general education classroom: Individualized instruction

Comments: R has done a good job in English. He participates regularly and completes all assignments on time. There are days when he doesn't want to work at all and it is really hard to get him started. He sometimes makes flippant comments that can seem disrespectful. He often works too quickly and makes avoidable errors. He has great ideas, but writing assignments are difficult for him.

Continued

Figure 3.2 / Sample Classroom-Based Assessment for a Secondary Student (continued)

Teacher	Subject	Period	Completion of Class Curriculum	Class Participation	Behavior Control
MF	STUDY SKILLS	6	Above Average	Average	Average
	Attendance	**Motivation**	**Interactions with Adults**	**Interactions with Peers**	**Current Grade**
	Average	Below Average	Average	Below Average	B

Accommodations used/needed in the general education classroom: Individualized course

Comments: R's behavior has been good during his Study Skills time, and he generally does a good job of using his time wisely. An area for improvement would be in using his assignment notebook consistently and doing what needs to be done without being pushed by adults.

Teacher	Subject	Period	Completion of Class Curriculum	Class Participation	Behavior Control
MF	FOODS	7	Above Average	Above Average	Average
	Attendance	**Motivation**	**Interactions with Adults**	**Interactions with Peers**	**Current Grade**
	Average	Average	Average	Below Average	C

Accommodations used/needed in the general education classroom: Individualized course

Comments: R is doing fine in Foods. He often volunteers to read out loud and participates regularly in class discussions. He seems to have a good base knowledge of kitchen safety and procedure. He does not seem very comfortable with his peers and tends to avoid interacting with them.

Teacher	Subject	Period	Completion of Class Curriculum	Class Participation	Behavior Control
CL	LIFE SKILLS MATH	5	Average	Average	Average
	Attendance	**Motivation**	**Interactions with Adults**	**Interactions with Peers**	**Current Grade**
	Below Average	Average	Average	Below Average	B-

Accommodations used/needed in the general education classroom: Special education support in the classroom, help outside of the class from special educator

Comments: Early absences caused R to fall behind. He also had difficulty speaking to peers.

Teacher	Subject	Period	Completion of Class Curriculum	Class Participation	Behavior Control
JS	WOODSHOP	4	Below Average	Below Average	Average
	Attendance	**Motivation**	**Interactions with Adults**	**Interactions with Peers**	**Current Grade**
	Average	Below Average	Below Average	Below Average	B

Accommodations used/needed in the general education classroom: Additional time for assignments, preferential seating, special education support in the classroom

Comments: On the following scale (terrible, bad, OK, good, great) I would rate R's performance as OK. R has good attendance and does average on all of his traditional academic assignments. His work performance in the shop to this point is a little below average. Two areas most needing attention are motivation and responsibility. To assist in these areas, I will encourage him to do a good job and help to instill a can-do attitude. On the responsibility part, I will hold him accountable for his assigned work to meet classroom expectations. I believe R is capable and able to be successful in the shop if he chooses to apply more effort.

(or a regular classroom teacher qualified to teach a student of his or her age if the student does not have a regular teacher) or, for a student younger than school age, an individual qualified to teach the student and at least one person qualified to conduct individual diagnostic examinations of students, such as a school psychologist.

What must the team consider?

To determine if a student has a disability and needs special education, a school district must gather information from a variety of sources, including aptitude and achievement tests, parent input, teacher recommendations, physical condition, social or cultural background, and adaptive behavior. As noted earlier, each disability category has specific criteria for qualifying a student, and within these criteria, states also often list the factors that would *exclude* a student from qualifying. The team uses the assessment information to determine if the student meets the criteria for that disability. Here is one particular state's criteria for identifying a learning disability:

1. A team may determine that a student has a specific learning disability if—
   - The student does not achieve commensurate with his or her age and ability levels in one or more of the areas listed below, if provided with learning experiences appropriate for the student's age and ability levels; and
   - The student has a severe discrepancy between achievement and intellectual ability in one or more of the following areas: oral expression; listening comprehension; written expression; basic reading skill; reading comprehension; mathematics calculation; mathematics reasoning; and/or a presented portfolio, and/or teacher reports on daily work which shows academic performance is not in an acceptable range.
2. The team may not identify a student as having a specific learning disability if the severe discrepancy between ability and achievement is primarily the result of—
   - A visual, hearing, or motor impairment;
   - Intellectual disability;
   - Emotional disturbance; or
   - Environmental, cultural, or economic disadvantage.
3. *Observation*—At least one team member other than the child's regular teacher shall observe the child's academic performance in the regular classroom setting.

4. *Written report*—For a child suspected of having a specific learning disability, the documentation of the team's determination of eligibility must include a statement of—

- Whether the child has a specific learning disability;
- The basis for making the determination;
- The relevant behavior noted during the observation of the child;
- The relationship of that behavior to the child's academic functioning;
- The educationally relevant medical findings, if any;
- Whether there is a severe discrepancy between achievement and ability that is not correctable without special education and related services; and
- The determination of the team concerning the effects of environmental, cultural, or economic disadvantage.

How does the law define a student with a disability?

IDEA, the federal law that governs special education, defines a child with a disability as follows:

> A student evaluated according to IDEA as having an intellectual disability, a hearing impairment (including deafness), a speech or language impairment, a visual impairment (including blindness), a serious emotional disturbance (referred to in IDEA as "emotional disturbance"), an orthopedic impairment, autism, traumatic brain injury, another health impairment, a specific learning disability, deaf-blindness, or multiple disabilities, and who, by reason thereof, needs special education and related services.

Why would a student not qualify?

Despite all the work done by the pre-referral team to rule out problems before a student is assessed, not every student who is referred for testing is found eligible for special education. Although you now have the benefit of a lot of additional information about the student's strengths and weaknesses that could help with instructional planning, the student will not be able to receive special education services to help with the problems that have shown up in the classroom.

There are potentially several reasons why the student might be found not eligible for special education. First, to be found eligible, students must have both a disability and need specially designed instruction. Some students have a disability but do not require the use of a special education teacher (see Chapter 5 for more information about these students).

Second, the student may not have met the criteria for one of the disability categories, even though he continues to struggle in school.

Third, maybe the interventions you tried have helped ameliorate the earlier issues so that the student is now performing well in the classroom. This kind of change in performance is actually fairly common. The effort may not get as far as the stage of formal testing, but a teacher's growing awareness of issues and problems, followed by providing an intervention and gathering data on that intervention, can often go a long way toward helping some students and preventing them from needing additional assistance from a special education teacher.

Fourth, students are eligible for special education only if they demonstrate problems *in school*. They may have a multitude of issues and problems at home, but if these are not adversely affecting the student's education, the student would not be found eligible. Often this situation is what triggers parents' requests for testing. More often than not, it is good practice to seriously consider parents' requests for an evaluation for special education. The parents may be concerned about issues they are seeing both in school reports and also at home, and in the end, an evaluation may help rule out issues for the student's education. It is important to note that if a district denies a parent's request for an evaluation and it is later found that the student has a disability, the district could potentially be open to a claim for loss of services.

Fifth, the student may have qualified for special education services but the parents did not allow the student's participation. Parents have the right to deny consent for services before such services begin, or, once a student is receiving services, parents may revoke consent for special education. If either of these situations occurs, the student must be treated like any other general education student; he or she is no longer afforded the rights and protections of a student with a disability.

Meeting the Criteria for Learning Disability: The Discrepancy Model Versus RTI

Increasingly states are moving toward identifying students for the category of learning disabilities using Response to Intervention and Multi-Tiered System of Supports, which we introduced in Chapter 2. Some districts still use the discrepancy formula (also introduced in Chapter 2), in which a "significant" discrepancy is found between where a student is performing and where that student could be performing based on ability.

Since 1978, the primary means of assessing students for eligibility in the category of learning disabilities has been through the discrepancy model. The discrepancy model is based on using students' IQ scores versus school performance to determine whether they are eligible for special education services. If there is enough difference between level of performance and where we would expect the student to be performing, then the student would be found to have a learning disability. The problems with this approach include a heavy reliance on IQ scores and the need to wait until there is a wide enough gap between where the student is functioning and the student's expected level of performance (Brown-Chidsey & Steege, 2010). Potentially, students might wait several years before they are eligible for special education and related services in the category of learning disabilities, which accounts for why the discrepancy model is often called the "wait to fail" approach (Brown-Chidsey & Steege, 2010). In recognition of this problem, IDEA stipulates the following:

1. States must not require use of significant discrepancy as part of the determination of a specific learning disability.

2. States must permit the use of a process based on a child's response to scientifically based intervention as part of the determination of a specific learning disability.

Parents' Rights Revisited

In Chapter 1 we covered in detail parents' rights relating to special education. Here is a quick reminder of the rights parents have relating to the evaluation process:

- The district has to obtain written parental permission before the formal assessment process can begin.
- Parents are to be provided information about the assessments that will be used.
- Parents have the right to revoke permission at any time during the process.
- Parents have the right to be included in the evaluation process.
- Parents have the right to obtain an independent educational evaluation if they disagree with the results of the evaluation completed by the school district.
- If parents disagree with the results of the evaluation conducted by the school district, they have the right to obtain an independent educational evaluation (IEE) at the district's expense. When parents request an IEE, the school must provide them with information about where they can obtain such an evaluation. The district must then consider the results of that evaluation.

3. States may permit the use of other alternative research-based procedures to determine whether a child has a specific learning disability (IDEA, 2004).

The Evaluation Report as a Tool for Planning Instruction

The evaluation report generated by the district contains a summary of all the assessments completed by the various people on the multidisciplinary team. You can learn a number of things from the report that can potentially help you with your instructional planning for the student who was tested. As you review the various sections of the report, keep an eye out for information about the following important topics.

Academic performance

The report summarizes the student's academic performance based not only on the information you provided but also on the results of formal standardized assessments. These results come from individually administered assessments and include standard scores that can give you a very clear idea of where the student is functioning compared with results on national norm-referenced tests. You can also use this assessment information to detect patterns in how the student processes information and for specific deficit areas. For example, does the student score lower on timed subtests, or does the student do well in understanding math concepts but not as well when multiplication is involved?

Psychological findings

The IQ test results can give you an idea of the student's intellectual functioning and an indication of how the student processes information. For example, you may learn that a student is better able to process information when it is presented visually, or that the student may need memory supports or more time to process information. IQ scores have a mean of 100, with most states using a cut-off for giftedness of about 130 and a cut-off for intellectual disability of about 70.

Social/emotional/behavioral findings

The results from assessments related to social/behavioral issues provide information describing the relationships the student has with others and how the student deals with interpersonal issues. For example, results may indicate the student needs instruction in self-regulating emotions, is highly distractible, or would benefit from instruction in appropriate social interactions with others.

Communication skills

The results in this area, which are usually addressed by a speech language pathologist, would indicate either difficulties in articulation or other broad language issues. For students who have difficulty communicating their thoughts or ideas to others or whose speech is difficult for you to understand, the assessment results would help determine appropriate individual services needed, or accommodations and modifications that would assist the student in the school environment.

Physical challenges

Assessment results would indicate how physical challenges are interfering with the student's educational performance, and they would most likely result in suggestions for modification and accommodations to be implemented in the general education classroom and, possibly, the need for consultative, collaborative, or direct services from a physical or occupational therapist.

Assistive technology recommendations

The team that develops the IEP makes decisions about assistive technology devices and services based on students' unique needs so that they can access and be more independent in their education program. The law requires schools to use assistive technology devices and services "to maximize accessibility for children with disabilities" (20 U.S.C. 1400(5)(H)). Assistive technology service is defined as

> any service that directly assists a child with a disability in the selection, acquisition, or use of an assistive technology device. Such term includes—(A) the evaluation of the needs of such child . . . ; (B) purchasing, leasing, or otherwise providing for the acquisition of assistive technology devices by such child; (C) selecting, designing, fitting, customizing, adapting, applying, maintaining, repairing, or replacing assistive technology devices; (D) coordinating and using other therapies, interventions, or services with assistive technology devices . . . ; (E) training or technical assistance for such child, or, where appropriate, the family of such child; and (F) training or technical assistance for professionals. . . . (20 U.S.C. 1401(2))

Classroom-based assessment

The evaluation will include a description of how the student performs in the general education classroom, based not only on the information you have provided but also on information from the person who observes the student in the classroom. Read this section carefully for any hints or suggestions for things like seating, grouping, or providing correction or reinforcement strategies that you could use to help this student and others in the classroom.

What to Do If the Student Is Not Eligible

Make sure you attend the meeting where the evaluation report is discussed; remember, you are a required team member. It is at this meeting that the student is found either eligible or not for special education. If the student is not found eligible, make sure you ask for specific suggestions during the meeting to help you with instruction in your general education classroom. There could be a lot of professional expertise in the room. Use the collective knowledge to help make plans for the student.

If a student is found to be not eligible for special education and related services, it is still important to carefully review the comprehensive team report, which details any issue the student may have from a variety of perspectives. Most of the students in your class do not have this kind of intense scrutiny and information provided about them. Read the report for suggestions that you can follow about programming and instruction as they specifically relate to the needs of the student.

Finally, do not stop trying to improve the student's educational experience. Continue to work to identify problem areas, gather data, and implement interventions.

Summary

The referral and evaluation process determines whether a student is eligible for special education and related services. A multidisciplinary team, of which the general education teacher is a required member, makes this determination after reviewing extensive data about the student's performance (including the student's response to any interventions that may have been implemented during the pre-referral stage) and the results of recommended assessments. A student is eligible for special education services only after the team has determined that the student meets the specific definitions of a student with a disability and requires specially designed instruction. Whether or not the student is found to be eligible, the detailed evaluation report provides valuable information that can be useful for providing effective instruction for the student. Understanding the referral and evaluation process and the role that you, as the general education teacher, have in this process will go a long way toward helping students with disabilities—and those without.

4

General Education Teachers and IEPs

In this chapter we define and discuss the individualized education program, commonly known as the IEP and its components, focusing on the role of the general education classroom teacher as it relates to each element, as well as important things to be aware of. We conclude with a series of checklists that will help you know what to do before, during, and after an IEP meeting.

What Is an IEP?

An individualized education program (also referred to as an "individualized education plan") is the written map for a student's education for the coming year, and it includes services beyond those offered to all students in the general education program. It is a formal document that is developed only after a student has been found eligible for special education and related services by a multidisciplinary team (as discussed in Chapter 3). The IEP is a legal document and a contract between the school and the parents outlining what services will be provided.

The IEP's multiple purposes

The IEP document itself is important because it records the specific plan the team has developed. The document can be used for several purposes, each of which we describe here. These purposes are not necessarily separate from each other and in many ways are interconnected.

Communication. The IEP document is a tool that all team members, including the parents, can refer to as a reminder of the plan that was agreed upon. It also serves as a tool that the multidisciplinary team can use to communicate with the various other education professionals (discussed in Chapter 1) who provide the services and support that the student is expected to receive, and it outlines who is responsible for what services.

Annual performance goals. The IEP lists goals and objectives that should be reasonable for the student to achieve over the next year. These goals are based on the student's present level of functioning, and they drive the special education services for the student.

Services provided. The IEP lists specific services a student is to receive. For example, if the student is expected to receive self-care instruction by a special education teacher, the instruction would be listed in the IEP, along with the frequency and duration of the service. Similarly, if the student is expected to receive two hours of reading and language arts instruction in a special education setting, or if a student is to receive special services for transportation to and from school, these are outlined in the IEP document.

Evaluation. The IEP document allows the IEP team to determine if the student is making progress. (See the text on page 67 for a description of the IEP team.) For each goal area, the IEP documents the student's current level of functioning and sets goals based on that level. During the year, the parents are informed of the student's progress toward those goals. The following year, when a new IEP is written, the student's level of function is again documented. It should be easy to see the improvement in functioning when comparing the IEPs from one year to the next.

Management. Administrators can refer to the IEP as a management tool when they are planning the allocation of staff and resources. Some students may require intensive supports in order to function in school, whereas others may require only minimal

IMPORTANT POINTS

- The IEP is the cornerstone of the educational services provided to students who receive special education services.

- An IEP has many components, each of which is important in helping the student receive an appropriate education.

- The IEP should be viewed and treated as a contract between the school district and the parents.

- The general education classroom teacher is responsible for implementing the accommodations, the modifications, and the instruction the student receives in the general education classroom.

- The general education classroom teacher plays an important role in the development of the IEP and is the curriculum expert on the multidisciplinary team.

- The general education teacher should come to the IEP meetings ready to discuss the student, the general education curriculum, and accommodations and modifications that the student may need to be successful.

- IEPs are reviewed at least annually.

supports. The administrators need to allocate district resources to ensure these supports are provided. The IEP document is a tool that they can rely on to help them plan appropriately. Teachers can also use the document as a management tool to help them plan for the amount of instructional time necessary to assist a student in mastering a goal or an objective, to set up the structure of the room, and to plan instruction to meet the student's needs.

Accountability. The district needs to ensure that the program the IEP team developed and agreed upon is implemented, and this document assists with that. Goals and objectives that are written into the IEP are the heart of the document. The district must make a good-faith effort to ensure that a student makes progress on those goals. The IEP, in part, holds the district accountable. If the student does not make progress on the designated goals, the district should reconvene the IEP team to arrange to either change the level of supports provided to the student, or change the specific goals being addressed.

Compliance and monitoring. Because districts receive state and federal funding for special education programs, a compliance-monitoring process is in place to ensure that the school district is, in fact, complying with state and federal regulations regarding the services provided to students with disabilities. During this monitoring, the IEP document is reviewed and is used to document that these regulations are being met.

The IEP as a contract

The IEP is a legally binding document and should be viewed as a contract between the school district and the parents. Schools must follow what is written in the IEP, which means that if, for example, the IEP team determines that a student needs special transportation to and from school, transportation would be listed in the IEP and the school district must then provide it. A district that does not provide the student with this transportation would be violating the contract and giving the parents the right to contest it. The same principle applies if a student is expected to receive accommodations and special education services for reading and the school district either does not provide them or provides them only occasionally. If the district fails to provide what is listed in the IEP, the parents can pursue litigation to get services reinstated (see Chapter 1 for more on parents' rights).

As a contract, the IEP can change as long as both parties (school district and parents) agree to the changes. If there is no agreement to make changes, the contract as originally written stands, and no changes can be made unless a court rules otherwise.

The IEP Team

The IEP team consists of various individuals, some of whom may have a dual role. Most IEP teams will include the following:

> **Typical Members of the IEP TEAM:**
>
> - The student
> - Parents or guardians
> - The general education teacher
> - A principal or administrator
> - A school psychologist or educational diagnostician

- The *student,* who helps identify his or her unique needs and areas for support. Typically, a student under age 16 is not required to be present, but good practice recommends including younger students in at least parts of the meeting.
- *Parents or guardians,* who can offer insight about the student's life outside the school setting, including areas of strength and weakness, interests, and concerns.
- The *general education teacher,* who provides valuable insight on expectations for the student regarding the standard curriculum, interactions with other students, the daily schedule, and other interventions.
- The *special education teacher,* who discusses instructional strategies, adaptations, and the amount of time necessary to implement the goals.
- A *local education agency representative* (likely a principal or other administrator), who is familiar with resources available at other agencies and can commit resources to meet IEP goals.
- *A person qualified to interpret evaluation results* (likely a school psychologist or an educational diagnostician), who interprets the evaluation results to help design instructional goals and objectives, including accommodations that might be necessary.

Some IEP teams will include the following individuals, on an "as needed" basis:

- A *speech language pathologist* to recommend tools, devices, and supports relating to communication.
- A *physical therapist (PT) or occupational therapist (OT)* to offer supports related to fine- and gross-motor skills.
- An *audiologist* to offer support and suggestions to ensure adequate hearing and communication capability for students with hearing loss.

Required Components of the IEP

An IEP may seem like a lot of paperwork, especially when it becomes 30 or 40 pages long. But each component of the IEP serves a purpose in helping the professionals working with the student to better understand what is needed and, as noted earlier, in communicating between school staff and parents, so that informed educational decisions can be made.

In this section we list and describe the components of the IEP and, where appropriate, briefly explain the rationale for a component. We include both components that are mandated by federal regulations and those that are typically found in most states' IEPs. Your state may have a different organizational framework, may call the components by different names, and may have other components not included in this section.

Demographics

This component lists the identifying information about the student, which may include name, date of birth, age, grade, anticipated year of graduation, school district, parents' names, address, phone number, and disability category.

IEP team signatures

Depending on your state, this section is where you and the other team members sign your names to indicate attendance and participation in the IEP meeting.

Notice of procedural safeguards

Parents are to be provided with a copy of the procedural notice, clarifying their rights, at least once a year. This section is where they write their signatures to indicate they have received a copy. It is important to get the parents to sign and date this verification that they have received a copy of the notice so the district has documentation of complying with this requirement.

Special considerations

Several questions must be asked as a part of the IEP, and if any are answered in the affirmative, the IEP needs to include programming related to that issue. These questions are often asked at the first part of the IEP meeting and usually are dispensed with quickly. They include the following:

1. Is the student blind or visually impaired?
2. Is the student deaf or hard of hearing?
3. Does the student have communication needs?
4. Does the student require assistive technology devices or services?
5. Does the student have limited English proficiency?
6. Does the student exhibit behaviors that impede his or her learning or that of others?

Present levels of performance

This component drives the implementation and development of the IEP, because all goals and objectives are based on the statements included here. This section summarizes the student's performance in the current educational program and indicates the student's instructional and functional levels. It includes information regarding classroom performance and the results of any academic achievement or functional performance assessments that have been administered. Information contained in this section provides baseline data for developing the IEP and writing measurable annual goals. The information in this section should consider the most recent results of the initial multidisciplinary team report or the most recent evaluation, curriculum-based assessments, and ongoing progress monitoring, as well as why it is important that the student improve in this area and how the student's performance compares to that of peers. The information should be stated in clear and concrete terminology. Here is an example of a Present Levels of Performance statement:

> Math is an area of strength for Ricky. He completes work carefully and neatly. He asks questions when he doesn't understand a problem. On a Skills checklist (August 2015), Ricky indicated that math is one of the three things that he is best at. In September 2015, Ricky completed the Brigance Transition Skills Inventory. In the math section, he completed 83% of addition problems, 67% of subtraction, 50% of multiplication, and 0% of division problems correctly. He read 100% of number words and numerals correctly, but completed 0% of the fraction and decimal operations accurately. His midterm grade report (October 2015) shows that he currently has a *B-* in his Life Skills Math course. Ricky's peers are able to independently perform higher-level mathematical operations. Ricky needs to build stronger math skills so he can complete his high school math curriculum and perform functions of daily living.

Goals and objectives

Annual goals are statements describing reasonable and measurable expectations of what a student should be able to accomplish over a calendar year. These statements should include specifics about the behaviors you want the student to perform (in reading, math, handwriting, speech, etc.) and how well you want the student to perform these actions. There needs to be a clear and direct link between the student's present level of performance and the goals and objectives. Here is an example of this component:

Measurable Annual Goal: Heather will use money accurately in a money situation/simulation with 80 percent accuracy as measured by an assessment administered every other month.

Short-Term Objectives:

- Given a random set of 20 coins, Heather will be able to sort the coins into like piles (for example "put all quarters together," etc.) independently with 80 percent accuracy as documented on an assessment administered every other month.
- Given a set of four coins, Heather will be able to place the coins in order of value from largest to smallest with 100 percent accuracy as measured by an assessment administered every other month.
- Given a 1-, a 5-, a 10-, and a 20-dollar bill, Heather will be able to identify the bill by dollar value ("five dollars") with 80 percent accuracy as measured by an assessment administered every other month.
- Given a 1-, a 5-, a 10-, and a 20-dollar bill, Heather will be able to place the bills in order of value from largest to smallest with 100 percent accuracy as measured by an assessment administered every other month.

The IEP team should write goals and objectives relating only to areas in the general education curriculum where the student needs special education services, and not those areas where the student is not expected to receive special education.

The IEP should state how often progress on the goals and objectives will be measured and how often the progress reports will be provided to the parents. Parents should receive progress notes on the IEP goals at least as often as general education parents receive report cards.

Accommodations and/or modifications

This section details any adaptation to content, methodology, or the delivery of instruction that assists the student in meeting the goals. The IEP team is expected to develop this component based on the student's individual needs, with consideration as to how the disability affects the student's ability to perform. This is a very important section for you as the general education teacher, because you will be providing much input on what should be included in this section, and you will be implementing its provisions.

That said, you should understand an important distinction between accommodations and modifications. An *accommodation* is a strategy that allows the student to work around the disability but does not change the content of the instruction—for example, allowing the student to give oral instead of written answers or allowing the student more time to complete a task. A *modification* is something more tangible and involves a change in the content, curriculum, or task so the student is able to be successful.

Necessary supports for the general education teacher

General education teachers providing support to students with a disability

> **Typical Accommodations and Modifications Found in an IEP**
>
> - Frequent checks for understanding
> - Directions clarified and repeated regularly
> - Extra time for assignments involving reading or writing
> - Notes provided if student makes an attempt
> - Preferential seating to support vision
> - Work/projects/tests can be taken to resource room after instruction
> - Tests modified to provide word bank, matching, or multiple-choice formats
> - Test essay questions modified for length or dictated to scribe
> - Student allowed time to journal, do breathing exercise, use a stress ball, or take time out
> - Student allowed to access resource room if coping skills not working
> - Behavior plan as needed

may need assistance in implementing the IEP—for example, in implementing speech goals, providing reading assistance, or implementing accommodations. This section of the IEP delineates the specific supports or training necessary for school personnel to deliver the free appropriate public education (FAPE) to which the student is entitled. These could include the following:

• *Aids*—Learning aids or behavioral tracking aids to help the student make it through the day

• *Resource materials*—Journal articles and other reading materials; websites that can help the teacher understand how to work better with the student's disability

• *Training*—Workshops on behavior management, new reading techniques, or new ways of gathering data so others can help with planning

• *Equipment*—Data-tracking software, apps for mobile devices that help gather data, or adaptive equipment that helps the student participate in the classroom

For each form of support, the IEP should list the school personnel who will receive the support and, if applicable, where (location) and how frequently they will receive it. The IEP must also specify the duration of the support—the anticipated beginning and ending dates.

Related services

If the IEP team determines the student needs a related service, the specifics of the frequency, location, and duration of the service, along with the beginning and ending dates, are included here. (See Chapter 8 for more information on related services.)

Participation in state assessments

As a result of the reauthorization of IDEA in 1997 and the Every Student Succeeds Act of 2015, students with disabilities are expected to participate in state assessments to determine annual progress using standardized measures. This section of the IEP discusses the extent of the accommodations the student is to receive, if any. These accommodations allow the student to participate in the assessment so that the results reflect the student's actual knowledge and not the effects of the disability. Alternative assessments are also available for students with disabilities who are functioning at a level significantly below that of the general population.

Placement

The needs of the student determine the goals and objectives that must be addressed, and the effort and time involved in addressing these goals and objectives determine the location of the services the student is to receive. Special education is a service, not a place, and the IEP team determines the placement for the services based on the student's needs, not on what is administratively available.

Transition

Depending on the state, decisions about postsecondary transition needs are to be addressed for the student by age 16 (age 14 in some states). The team develops a "coordinated set of activities . . . to facilitate the child's movement from school to post-school activities, including postsecondary education, vocational training, integrated employment (including supported employment), continuing and adult education, adult services, independent living, or community participation" (IDEA, 2004). (For more information about transition for students with disabilities, see Chapter 6.)

Your Role in Developing the IEP

Typically either a special education teacher or a special education administrator writes the IEP, based on information they have gathered from team members. This does not mean a general education teacher does not have an important role in the development of the student's IEP. In fact, as the general education teacher, you should consider yourself the curriculum expert on the team. You will provide valuable information regarding the curriculum that is taught in your class, the accommodations and modifications that may be needed, the social interactions of the student across school settings, how this student's performance compares with that of peers, and what specific skills are imperative for the student to learn in order to be successful in the general education setting or to move forward in the curriculum. You will have gathered some of this information during the classroom assessments described in Chapter 3, and you should be prepared to present it to the IEP meeting each year and to provide it to the developer of the IEP itself. Although it is not required by law, we highly recommend that general education teachers come prepared to present this information to the IEP team. The importance of your role in ensuring that students receive the services they need cannot be overstated.

Now we would like to turn to components of the IEP that directly affect you in your role as the general education teacher.

Least restrictive environment

In Chapter 1 we identified least restrictive environment (LRE) as one of the eight core principles of special education. Under LRE, the presumption is that students with disabilities will be educated in general education classrooms alongside their typically learning peers as much as possible and provided with the necessary supports and services to meet their needs. Students with disabilities are to participate fully, both academically and socially. In addition, as the general education teacher, you are expected to differentiate the methods used in providing services so all students will benefit from instruction.

Students with disabilities are to be educated in the general education classroom until all available methods have been tried to meet their needs in this environment. Only after every reasonable method has been tried and the student's needs have not been met should the student be pulled out for additional services. Examples of this kind of pull-out include students being briefly removed to get help with a specific reading problem and then going back to the general education classroom when they have mastered a skill, or students with emotional issues being taught strategies for dealing with frustration and then returning to the general education classroom. Figure 4.1 shows a schedule for one student's special education services that will be provided outside the general education classroom.

Figure 4.1 / Sample Schedule for Special Education Services

Special Education or Related-Service Area	Education Setting	Total Minutes per Week	Dates of Service
Math	Special education setting	250.0	10/26/2016–10/25/2017
Written Expression	Special education setting	250.0	10/26/2016–10/25/2017
Social/Emotional/ Behavioral	Special education setting	100.0	10/26/2016–10/25/2017
Self-Help/ Independence	Special education setting	400.0	10/26/2016–10/25/2017
Total Minutes:		1,000	

What is not acceptable is placing a student in a special education class without even trying accommodations, or automatically assuming a student needs assistance just because of the presence of a disability. Case law on this is very specific: removal to a special education classroom is done only after other options have been tried. See, for example, *Daniel R. R. v. State*

Board of Education (1989); *Oberti v. Board of Education of the Borough of Clementon School District* (1993); and *Roncker v. Walter* (1983).

Accommodations versus modifications

Earlier in this chapter we briefly discussed accommodations and modifications as a component of the IEP. As a general education classroom teacher, you will hear a lot of discussion about accommodations and modifications, and although the terms refer to similar things, as we noted previously, they are not synonyms. The difference between the two is worth further explanation.

Accommodations change how a student learns the material. An accommodation allows a student to complete the same assignment or test as other students, but with a change in the timing, formatting, setting, scheduling, response, presentation, or a combination of these. The accommodation does not alter in any significant way what the test or assignment measures. For example, accommodations for *presentation* affect the way directions and content are delivered to students, helping students with different learning needs and abilities to engage in the content (e.g., a student with a vision problem might listen to an audio recording of a text). Accommodations for *response* offer different ways for students to respond to assessment questions. Accommodations for *setting* typically affect where work or specific tasks are completed; a change of setting may be particularly helpful to students who are easily distracted. Accommodations for *timing* and *scheduling* of assignments and assessments can be helpful for students who may need more processing time or frequent breaks.

Modifications change what a student is taught or expected to learn. Notably, they are adjustments to an assignment or a test that change the standard of what the assignment or test is supposed to measure. The curriculum can be modified to retain specific standards that the student must meet to progress in the curriculum, while allowing for less depth of understanding of the concept.

Figure 4.2 shows some examples of accommodations and modifications for both academic and behavioral expectations.

Suggesting and providing for appropriate accommodations and modifications constitute a major function of the general education teacher when planning and implementing the IEP. Appendix D has additional information about accommodations and modifications, and Appendix E lists other examples of modifications.

Figure 4.2 / Examples of Accommodations and Modifications

Expectations	Accommodations	Modifications
Academic	• Providing vocabulary lists for reading material • Pairing with a more advanced reading buddy • Providing an outline of chapter content or presentation notes • Providing a list of discussion questions before class • Providing reading materials in Braille	• Providing a shorter list of spelling words to study for the week • Providing reading materials at a lower grade level • Grading on effort or participation • Providing a word bank for fill-in-the-blank questions
Behavioral	• Rewarding positive behavior • Pairing with a buddy who models good behavior • Using of nonverbal cues or code words to communicate inappropriate behavior • Changing seating arrangements to make it easier to concentrate	• Allowing for shorter periods of on-task behavior • Waiving "out-of-seat" rules

Participation in state and district assessments

As the general education classroom teacher, you can provide valuable information to the IEP team on appropriate and necessary accommodations for students with disabilities related to their participation in state and districtwide assessments. Because you probably know the student better than any other educational professional, you can advocate on the student's behalf. Under IDEA, students with disabilities must have access to the general education curriculum and should have access to those courses tested by the state assessments. The IEP team makes the determination about a student's participation in academic courses, as well as the assessments that are used.

For students who qualify to participate in an alternate assessment system, the IEP must include an explanation of why the student cannot participate in the statewide assessments. The IEP also must explain why the alternative is an appropriate assessment for the student. Here is a list of questions to ask in determining appropriate accommodations for assessment:

• Are preferred accommodations allowed on state and district assessments of achievement?

• What accommodations increase the student's access to instruction and assessment?

• What accommodations has the student tried in the past?

• What has worked well, and in what situations?

• What does the student prefer?

• Does the student still need the accommodation?

• Are there ways to improve the student's use of the accommodation?

• Are there other accommodations that the student should try?

• Are there opportunities for the student to use the preferred accommodations on practice tests?

• What arrangements need to be made to make sure the student's preferred accommodations are available in assessment situations?

• How can actual use of accommodations be documented?

• What are the challenges of providing the student's preferred accommodations, and how can these be overcome?

Reevaluation

At least once every three years, or more frequently if needed or if the parent or teacher requests it, IEP teams must consider a reevaluation. The reevaluation has three purposes:

• To determine whether the student remains eligible for special education services

• To ensure the individual needs of a student with a disability are identified

• To gather information that is necessary for appropriate educational programming

No matter what the purpose, the team must consider if the student continues to meet the specified disability category. The team may determine that additional information is not needed for program planning and forgo the formal reevaluation process. However, the team may determine that they need additional information for program planning and can complete those assessments outside of the formal evaluation process for qualification for special education. Check with your special education administrator or special education teacher to see how this matter is handled in your state and district.

In the case of determining whether or not the student is still eligible for special education services, the decision must be documented. As the general education teacher who has worked most closely with the student, your role in the reevaluation process requires you to do the following:

- Share current classroom-based assessments and observations
- Share observations related to the student's work with other teachers and related-service providers
- Provide any other pertinent information (e.g., attendance data, health/medical reports, disciplinary record)
- Present your perspective as to whether you believe the student still has a disability and how the student relates to the other students in the class
- Share the strategies or program components that have been successful or unsuccessful for the student

When reviewing data, the team should also look at evaluations and information provided by the student's parents; observations by other teachers and related-service providers who have worked with the student; and results of state and district assessments. In some cases, the determination of a student's continued eligibility may require more testing.

Standards-Based IEPs

Increasingly common, a "standards-based IEP" considers how a student is currently performing compared to expected performance on grade-level academic standards and aims to bridge the gap and raise the student's level of functioning to grade level.

The obvious benefit of a standards-based IEP is its potential to help students stay on track for their grade. It can be a valuable tool to support coordinated instructional planning among the various members of the student's IEP team. On the other hand, using standards to establish IEP goals can ignore the individual needs of the student. Additionally, if the student is functioning significantly below grade level, moving the student to grade level may be very difficult.

The IEP Meeting

The agenda and content of IEP meetings vary from state to state and from district to district. Above all, they are based on the needs of the student, as well as the specific requirements of the state and the state forms that are used. That said, here is a summary of a "typical" IEP meeting:

• *Introductions*—It is customary to begin the meeting by having all participants introduce themselves and state how they are involved with the student.

• *Procedural safeguards*—Federal law requires that parents or guardians be given information about their procedural safeguards at least annually. Many districts ask for a signature certifying that the procedural safeguards have been received.

• *Strengths and concerns*—The team discusses the student's strengths and any areas of concern in a broad sense.

• *Previous goals*—The team reviews progress on the past year's goals.

• *Present levels of performance*—The team reviews a summary of the student's "present levels of academic achievement and functional performance." The summary should also include language about how the disability affects the student's ability to participate in the general curriculum. As the general education classroom teacher, you would be expected to report about the student's progress in your classroom.

• *Statement of proposed goals and objectives*—The team discusses proposed goals and objectives (academic and functional) to be included in the IEP.

• *Service times*—The team discusses how much time will be required to help the student reach the goals and objectives. It is important for you, as the general education teacher, to help clarify this aspect of assistance.

• *State and district assessments*—The team discusses the type and amount of accommodations the student will get while taking mandated state and district-level assessments (if any). As the general education teacher, you should speak about expectations regarding the student's performance on such assessments.

• *Placement*—The team discusses where the student will receive special education services, including consideration of access to typically developing peers.

• *Agreement*—In most states, agreement is demonstrated by having the parents sign the IEP document at the end of the meeting. This indicates support for the proposed program.

Four Important Points

By now we hope you understand that general education classroom teachers have a vital role in the development and implementation of a student's IEP.

Following up on all the information we have presented in this chapter, we would like to emphasize four important points.

First, as stated before, you are a key member of the IEP team. You are the one who typically refers the student for testing, and the one who works with the student every day and sees how the student is progressing in the curriculum and interacting with others. Your input is needed specifically in regard to the general education curriculum, use of accommodations and modifications, and participation in state and district assessments.

Second, because you are a key member of the team and will likely notice problems before others do, you can call for an IEP meeting to discuss issues at any time. It does not have to be a special education teacher or a principal who makes the request.

Third, it is very important for you to preserve confidentiality regarding all the information that is shared about the student. You are legally required to maintain confidentiality and to talk about the student only with those who need to know.

Fourth, at least one general education teacher is required to attend the IEP meeting. If possible, all general education teachers who work with the student should be present, not only to fully convey thoughts and ideas about the student to others, but also to understand what is expected of them in the implementation of the IEP. Those general education teachers who do not attend are still required to implement the IEP.

Summary

The IEP is the core document related to the provision of services for students with disabilities, and general education teachers play a key role in its development and implementation, because they are the ones who spend the most time with students, regularly observing their academic, social, and behavioral strengths and needs. General education teachers have important knowledge about content, what goes on in the classroom, the pace of lessons, instruction provided, and information on state standards—all of which are relevant to the IEP.

IEPs serve several purposes related to communication, accountability, compliance and monitoring, and management, as well as clarification of annual performance goals and specification of services to be provided. They should be viewed as a contract between the school district and the student's parents or guardians.

Some of the most important components of the IEP are a description of the student's current level of performance, goals and objectives for the coming year, accommodations and modifications that may be needed for the student to attain the goals and objectives, supports that may be needed for the teachers and other personnel who will be working with the student, a delineation of related services that may be required, and a description of the student's expected participation in state and district assessments.

At least one general education teacher is required to attend IEP meetings and is expected to share observations of the student and the student's needs as part of the development the IEP. The general education teacher is expected to provide descriptions of services, adaptations, and modifications required to help the student, as well as recommendations and feedback regarding the development of the IEP. Other IEP team members generally include the student, the parents or guardians, a school administrator, the special education teacher, and someone qualified to interpret evaluation results, such as a school psychologist or an educational diagnostician.

5

Other Students Who Require Accommodations

In this chapter we discuss three types of students who do not meet the requirements for special education but still require accommodations. We begin by explaining Section 504, a nondiscrimination law that applies to many students who have disabilities but do not qualify for special education services. We discuss gifted and talented students in recognition of the fact that they, too, have needs that are important to address. Finally, we consider students who are at risk for failure and may or may not be receiving additional assistance, discussing both classroom and schoolwide supports.

What You Need to Know About Section 504

In Chapter 1 we pointed out that some students with disabilities do not meet the qualifying criteria for special education and related services but may require some other types of services in order to have their needs met to the same degree as students without a disability. Support for these students is provided through Section 504, a brief but powerful nondiscrimination law included in the Rehabilitation Act of 1973 (PL 93-112). It extends to individuals with disabilities the same kinds of protections Congress extends to people discriminated against because of race and sex.

In the United States, all students have the right to a free public education. Section 504 ensures that students who have a disability that affects a major life function will continue to have access to that free public education despite their disability. A few common disabilities covered by Section 504 plans in schools include ADD/ADHD, nut allergies, and diabetes.

Here are additional important points related to Section 504:

• Section 504 is an antidiscrimination law. School districts receive no federal funds to implement this law.

• The responsibility not to discriminate against individuals with disabilities applies to all school personnel.

• In addition to students with disabilities, parents and employees also cannot be discriminated against.

• General education programs and staff have the primary responsibility for the implementation of Section 504. Staff from special education may be consulted, but they do not have responsibility for implementation of the accommodations for the student.

• The accommodations required by Section 504 apply to the entire school and extend to parents and visitors to events.

What is a Section 504 plan?

Similar to an IEP, a Section 504 plan lists the accommodations an eligible student would receive. It is individualized and based on the specific needs of the student's disability. Because an eligible student will receive these services through general education programs or general education–funded programs, it is very important that you, as the general education teacher, be a part of and understand the specific components of the plan.

Who qualifies for a Section 504 plan?

According to the U.S. Department of Education (2015b), "to be protected under Section 504, a student must be determined to: (1) have a physical or mental impairment that substantially limits one or more major life

IMPORTANT POINTS

• Not all students with a disability receive special education services; however, they may still be entitled to accommodations.

• Students with disabilities who do not receive special education services are the responsibility of the general education program.

• Section 504 covers students with disabilities who do not receive special education services but have needs based on a disability.

• Students eligible for Section 504 have many of the same rights as students identified as requiring special education services.

• Students who are gifted and talented may need accommodations to help with their academic programming.

Typical Qualifying Conditions for a Section 504 Plan

Physical Impairments

- AIDS and HIV
- Allergies
- Arthritis
- Cancer
- Cerebral palsy
- Diabetes
- Visual impairment
- Epilepsy
- Heart disease
- Hemophilia
- Temporary conditions (such as broken limbs) due to accident or illness
- Tourette syndrome

Mental Impairments

- ADD/ADHD
- Conduct disorders
- Depression
- Eating disorders
- Past drug/alcohol addiction

---

activities [learning is considered a major life activity]; or (2) have a record of such an impairment; or (3) be regarded as having such an impairment."

An important consideration in determining eligibility is clarifying the specific problem students might have that would qualify them for a 504 plan. Examples of substantial life functions that, if impaired, would trigger an individual's eligibility include breathing, walking, talking, seeing, hearing, learning, and taking care of oneself.

What does a Section 504 plan contain?

Whereas IEPs can run 30 to 40 pages, a Section 504 is fairly short—often only a page and a half long.

The main components of a Section 504 plan delineate the specific aids, services, and accommodations a student is expected to receive and the parties responsible. Some plans include more information, such as a description of the nature of the concern; evaluation information (identifying the student's specific disability); the basis for determining the disability; how the disability affects a major life activity; and a list of those who attended the meeting to develop and approve the plan.

For you, the general education teacher, the most important parts of the 504 plan are those referring to accommodations the student needs and the teacher's responsibilities when it comes to providing those accommodations. Figure 5.1 shows a sample Section 504 plan.

Figure 5.1 / Sample Section 504 Plan

SCHOOL DISTRICT

Street Address

City, State

504 Service Agreement

Student Name:_____ Grade: _____

Name of Parent/Guardian: _____ Parent/Guardian Phone:_____

School Building:_____ School Address:_____

Date of Initial Agreement: 10/23/2013   Date Services End: 9/24/2016

Date Agreement Was Modified: 9/24/2015

Disability/Impairment: ADHD

This plan summarizes our recent evaluation concerning your child and summarizes our recommendations and agreements for aids, services, or accommodations.

Aids, Services, Accommodations	Party Responsible
Student will receive preferential seating, in close proximity to teacher.	Teachers
Student's agenda will be signed daily.	Student/Teachers/ Parents
Directions/instructions will be provided in a simple, concise manner.	Teachers
Student will restate directions to ensure comprehension.	Student/Teachers
Teachers will provide subtle redirections/checks for understanding.	Teachers
Teachers and parents will communicate academic concerns.	Teachers/Parents/ Counselor
Student will be provided with both oral and written directions.	Teachers
Student will be encouraged to advocate for herself by asking for additional help/clarification where necessary.	Student
Student will receive small-group testing for standardized tests.	Teachers
Nurse will provide reminders for student to take midday medication. Nurse will call for student if she does not show up by 1:00.	Nurse

Figure 5.1 / Sample Section 504 Plan (continued)

The following procedures need to be followed in the event of a medical emergency:

_____

_____

_____

The attached letter outlines your rights to resolve any disputes you may have concerning the recommended aids, services, or accommodations. If you have any questions concerning your rights or the aids, services, or accommodations recommended, please feel free to contact the administrator who signed below.

Directions to the parents: Please initial one of the options and sign below.

_____ I agree and give permission to proceed as recommended.

_____ I do not agree and do not give permission to proceed as recommended.

_____ I would like to schedule an informal conference to discuss my concerns.

My reason for disapproval is: _____

_____

Parent's Signature: _____ Date: _____

The school district agrees to provide the accommodations recorded in this document.

*Administrator's Signature: _____ Date: _____

Administrator's Title: _____

Also in Attendance

_____

(*Signature here denotes attendance only and does not indicate agreement.*)

Name   Role   Signature

Note: The administrator's signature indicates that the district agrees to implement the conditions of the Service Agreement.

Who develops a Section 504 plan?

Different states, and even different schools within the same district, may have varying procedures for developing a Section 504 plan. Principals, school counselors, Section 504 coordinators, or school nurses may write a plan. In any case, it's critical that both an administrator and the general education teacher be involved in the process. The administrator's participation is important to ensure that funds are available for any necessary services.

What happens at a Section 504 plan meeting?

Again, the procedures followed can vary from state to state and within districts. However, the meeting should include the following components:

• *Introductions*—Everyone should introduce themselves and state how they are involved with the student.

• *A description of the concern*—Information about the concern that prompted the meeting may come from a physician, a psychologist, a parent, a teacher, or another individual who helps with diagnosis.

• *A review of the evaluation*—This information may be included in the discussion of the nature of the concern, and it should specify who did the evaluation and what the results were.

• *A discussion of the basis of determination*—Here, participants should focus on the evaluation results and how the disability affects the student's involvement in school.

• *A discussion of how the disability affects a major life activity*—This component may be part of the previous discussion on basis of determination. For example, if a student has an allergy to tree nuts, participants would discuss the fact that the student's exposure to tree nuts could result in a life-threatening allergic reaction.

• *A discussion of services needed*—The discussion should focus on what services the student will need, based on the disability, and who within the school will have primary responsibility for implementing the services. Often the Section 504 plan includes accommodations needed to ensure that the student's disability is not interfering with learning. Those accommodations are the responsibility of the general education teacher, although other school personnel may also have responsibility. For example, the school counselor could have some responsibility for working with a student who has depression.

What should you do to help a student with a Section 504 plan?

As a general education teacher, you have a primary responsibility for implementing the components of the Section 504 plan. Here is a list of steps to take to ensure you fulfill your role in ensuring the student's needs are fully addressed:

1. Read the Section 504 plan.
2. Ask questions about any areas of concern or ambiguity.
3. Talk with the student's parents about the needs specified in the plan and what should be done.
4. Talk with the student's previous teachers about what they did to implement the accommodations.
5. Talk with the student about the needs specified in the plan and the best ways to make sure the student receives the accommodations.
6. If there are problems with the student not participating in the plan or with the accommodations, let others know (for example, your building administrator) and reconvene a meeting to discuss the plan.

Who has oversight of Section 504 plans?

Every district should have one person who is ultimately responsible for development and monitoring of Section 504 plans. Large districts will likely have such a person in each building. This individual should be available to help with questions from either staff or parents about responsibilities and components of the actual Section 504 plans. In addition, in the event of grievances, this person will represent the district in response to any complaints.

What kinds of accommodations might a Section 504 plan include?

The necessary accommodations in the Section 504 plan depend on the student's specific disability and related needs. For example, students with diabetes may require frequent monitoring of their blood sugar levels, or a student with epilepsy may need appropriate response procedures to deal with various kinds of seizures. (For more information on accommodations and modifications, see Appendixes D and E.)

Helping Students with ADD/ADHD

Many students with attention deficit disorder (ADD)/attention deficit hyperactivity disorder (ADHD) have Section 504 plans. ADD/ADHD is a chronic condition affecting millions of children, and general education classroom teachers spend a lot of time implementing plans that address it. The plans are intended to deal with behaviors that a student might engage in that could distract the teacher and the other students in the class, in addition to any problems the student may have with matters such as following directions, staying organized, and completing tasks.

Characteristics of ADHD

The main characteristics of ADHD are inattention, hyperactivity, and impulsivity. These symptoms often appear early in a student's life. However, the condition is difficult to diagnose in young children, because all children have problems with inattention at some point. Either a medical professional or a child psychologist makes the diagnosis.

There are three main types of ADHD: the predominantly hyperactive-impulsive type, in which the child does not show significant inattention; the predominantly inattentive type (sometimes called ADD), in which the child does not show significant hyperactive-impulsive behavior; and the combined type, in which the child displays both inattentive and hyperactive-impulsive symptoms.

ADHD can manifest in different ways. Some students with ADHD seem to have boundless energy and can never sit still in the classroom; others seem to be always staring off into space and take several seconds to realize the teacher has called on them. Another important but often forgotten fact is that students with ADHD may sometimes seem to have an intense focus or drive to do something. Many general education teachers and parents falsely assume that this ability to focus intensely on one thing (for example, a video game) means that the student cannot have ADHD. In fact, such students may still be diagnosed with this disability.

Education professionals often focus on inattention or hyperactivity as the biggest problem confronting students with ADHD, but doing so shifts attention away from related problems the student might have, such as low self-esteem, serial relationships, and inconsistent or poor performance in school. ADHD seems to lessen as individuals become adults, but it may not necessarily go away completely.

Treatment

The medical professional who diagnoses a student as having ADD/ADHD may prescribe medication. In addition, treatment typically involves behavioral interventions. Although treatment doesn't cure ADD/ADHD, it can help a great deal with symptoms. Early diagnosis and treatment can make a big difference in outcomes.

As a general education teacher, you may play a role in assisting medical professionals with diagnosis by observing and providing data on a student's performance. Additionally, after a student has been diagnosed with ADD/ADHD and if medication has been prescribed, the doctor may contact you for a follow-up report on the student's performance. Medical professionals may send questionnaires or checklists for you to complete; of course, you should always be honest and complete these forms as promptly as possible. The amount of medication is based in part on weight and age, but some students need more or less than others, and your input can be valuable in determining correct dosage.

Educational considerations

Many students with ADD/ADHD have difficulty in school because school generally requires attention and the ability to delay impulses. Students with ADD/ADHD respond best in structured, predictable environments where rules and expectations are clear and consistent, and consequences are clear and immediately enforced. They may also benefit from adaptations that allow for more movement and frequent breaks from the need to pay close attention. They can also benefit from additional cues to keep on task. With structure, routines, and rules, students can learn strategies for controlling their own behavior and get the help they need for learning.

Eligibility and ADD/ADHD

We have included discussion of ADD/ADHD in this chapter because it is one of the most frequent issues a general education classroom teacher has to address. However, some students with ADD/ADHD may be eligible for special education. Chapter 3 included a detailed discussion of the process that determines a student's eligibility for special education and related services. You will recall that eligibility for special education has two components: the diagnosis of a disability and the need for specially designed instruction. By itself, a medical diagnosis of ADD/ADHD is not enough to make a student eligible for services; in addition to the diagnosis, educational performance—which includes social, emotional, behavioral, or academic performance—must be adversely affected. Students with ADD/ADHD who are found eligible for special education would be included under the category of Other Health Impaired. (Of course, some students with ADD/ADHD may be eligible under other disability categories as well.)

Gifted and Talented Students

Although you may think of "students with needs" primarily in terms of students who are not performing as well as their peers, most likely you also have students in your classroom who are gifted and talented, and they also have needs. Your state may or may not have special identification procedures or supports for gifted students; there is no federal mandate for the provision of services to gifted students, as there is for students with disabilities, because students who are gifted and talented are not a protected class that has been historically discriminated against (Davis, Rimm, & Siegle, 2010). However, keep in mind that you may have a gifted student who also has a disability, including a learning disability or a physical disability, or who is on the autism spectrum. The term used for this is *twice exceptional*.

Whereas the U.S. government specifies definitions of various disabilities (see Appendix B), there is no standard definition of giftedness. Generally speaking, giftedness includes students who have strong or superior abilities in the following areas:

- General intellect
- Academic aptitude
- Leadership
- Visual or performing arts
- Creativity

The definition of giftedness may seem abstract, and at first you may think that it does not apply to your students. But giftedness can be demonstrated in many different areas and in many different ways, so it is important to note the various characteristics that such students may display.

Characteristics

Not all students who are gifted display all (or even most) of the characteristics we describe here, so keep this in mind when you observe your students. Some of the characteristics are developmental, meaning that students may display a range of levels of functioning related to the characteristics, with some becoming more apparent as the student gets older. Finally, like other students in your classes, students who are gifted tend to do better when they are engaged in subjects or activities they find interesting. Therefore, do not assume that students who are gifted in reading, for example, will demonstrate superior abilities in all reading activities. They may differentiate themselves from others only on topics they find interesting.

Here are definitions and descriptions of some characteristics that a gifted student may display (Davis et al., 2010):

• *Concentration*—Students who are identified as gifted and talented tend to have the ability to concentrate on tasks for much longer periods than others, and to be able to focus on activities when others start to lose interest.

• *Memory*—One of the more noticeable characteristics of students who are gifted and talented is their ability to remember events from the past that others seem to have forgotten, along with details about events they have experienced.

• *Language*—Students who are gifted often demonstrate a strong ability to use and understand both verbal and written language.

• *Curiosity*—This characteristic is often paired with the concentration that gifted students demonstrate, but such students are often curious not only about the object in front of them but also about the history behind the object and how it may have evolved over time.

• *Variety of interests*—Although some students who are gifted may appear to have just one or two interests they are working to master, most have a range of interests they are exploring at any given time.

Recommended practices

The Association for the Gifted, a division of the Council for Exceptional Children, has a wealth of information related to providing services for students who are gifted and talented (see http://CECTAG.com). Many of the recommendations for working with students who are gifted relate to the three educational practices: curriculum compacting, acceleration, and enrichment (Callahan & Plucker, 2013).

Curriculum compacting. Most curriculum involves frequent and repeated exposure of content to the students. Science concepts covered in 3rd grade are repeated in more depth in 5th grade, and in even more depth in 7th grade. Gifted students can often learn the concepts with only one exposure and can remember the salient facts due to their levels of concentration and memory. Make sure district curriculum is covered, but provide opportunities for the students to extend their knowledge of the information.

Acceleration. Because of their ability to master material through curriculum compacting, gifted students can accelerate through the curriculum rather rapidly. As a result, some students might be exposed to 5th grade math in 3rd grade, for example, and a few might even skip a grade. They will not necessarily accelerate in every subject, however. For example, they may show great prowess in math, placing them several years ahead of their chronological peers, while functioning only slightly ahead of their peers in reading.

Enrichment. Enrichment allows for a student to learn more about the ideas and activities occurring in the general education classroom. For example, as the students in your math class are learning about the Pythagorean theorem, the students who are gifted could also be learning about Pythagoras of Samos—his life, the era in which he lived, and his other accomplishments.

The need for appropriate education

Although some states do not identify or keep track of the number of gifted students, it is still important that these students receive services and support; otherwise they may become bored, develop behavior problems or an aversion to school, or negatively affect the learning of other students in the classroom. Like all students, they need instruction that challenges them, and despite the apparent ease with which they grasp skills and knowledge, they still need someone to guide them through the important points and explain how skills and concepts relate to each other.

As noted earlier, students with disabilities can also be gifted. The difference is that students who are eligible for special education services can also receive instruction from the special education teacher, which gives you, as the general education classroom teacher, a colleague to work with to implement goals for these students.

Keep in mind that students who are gifted may receive poor grades. Yes, they may have superior intelligence, but this does not mean they paid attention to the lesson, were interested in the content, or understood the questions on the test. They may lose interest and may also hide their intelligence as a way of getting other students to pay attention to them (Callahan & Plucker, 2013).

Be careful about expecting gifted students to do the same educational activities over and over. Students who can complete a task quickly should not have to do more of the same. For example, a student who is able to complete 20 math problems in five minutes while everyone else needs the rest of the class period should not be asked to just do more of the same—which is, in effect, punishing the student for finishing quickly. Think about extension and enrichment activities for the student who has quickly demonstrated understanding of a concept.

Finally, most general education classrooms have a wide variety of students, and like students with disabilities, students who are gifted require additional attention. It may be tempting to just send them to the Internet to learn or extend their knowledge, but you will still need to work with them and challenge them to learn material beyond what the other students are learning in the classroom.

Students at Risk

In addition to students with disabilities (some qualifying for special education services and others for Section 504 plans) and students who are gifted and talented, your classroom likely has some students who are at risk for failure. Some may become eligible for special education and related services in the future, but many will not. They will likely need additional supports from you and other school staff to make it through their academic career.

The term "at risk" is used to describe students considered to have a higher probability of school failure or of dropping out of school. It may be applied to students who deal with issues affecting their ability to complete school, such as homelessness, incarceration (of either the student or a parent), pregnancy, health issues, domestic violence, or frequent moves. Academic issues can include students who have problems with learning disabilities, low test scores, repeating grades, or discipline. Students who are at risk are a concern for all educators.

Students can flow in and out of the at-risk category, which makes it difficult to pinpoint exact numbers in terms of prevalence. The at-risk category could be defined so broadly as to be almost meaningless, but the important point is that *every* student has issues that need to be addressed. The needs of a student who is at risk because of homelessness differ from those of a student who has health issues or those of a student who has seen or has had to deal with domestic violence. Each of these has an individual need, and each may be potentially considered at risk for school failure. It is important for every teacher to take these needs seriously.

In most cases, being at risk is situational rather than innate (Gargiulo, 2015). With the exception of characteristics such as having a disability, students' at-risk status is rarely related to their ability to learn or succeed academically, and is largely or entirely related to outside factors. Attending a low-performing school could be considered an at-risk factor (Brendtro, Brokenleg, & Van Bockern, 2009). In addition, underfunded schools could contribute to higher rates of course failures and problems with attrition (Brendtro et al., 2009).

Things to do for students at risk

Here are some general recommendations.

Individualize. Treat the student as an individual. As noted earlier, students who are at risk can have issues that differ from those of other students. For example, work with students who are homeless (or potentially homeless) on their specific needs, and do not make assumptions about their needs, even if you have worked with homeless students before.

Set expectations. Maintain high but obtainable expectations. Your goal in working with these students is to help them learn, not to add additional stresses to their life. However, for some of these students, school could be the most normal part of their day. Treat them as you would treat others, seeking to maintain the same expectations you have for others when possible. But pay close attention to assignments and the students' performance to ensure you are not adding stress.

Involve others. Make sure the principal, the assistant principal, and others in the building who work with the student are aware of the needs. Other professionals might be aware of resources that could benefit the student and family. Tap their knowledge. Realize there may be students in other grades with similar stressors and that resources or assistance might need to be provided to them as well.

Enlist school counselors. The school counselor could become a resource or confidant for the student on a variety of issues. Involving school counselors is a great way to obtain assistance and to make others aware of issues that might be contributing to problems in school performance that a student might have.

Work closely with the family when you can. Some families do not want others intruding on their issues. Be careful to respect their feelings and attitudes. Talk with a school counselor or principal about this. But when families want to be involved, listen to their concerns and ideas, and work with them to address their child's classroom needs to the best of your ability. Keep the family informed about progress and issues related to the student's school performance.

Maintain confidentiality. Share information only with others who need to know and who can help the student with the issues being addressed. Doing so helps to preserve the student's respect, dignity, and self-esteem.

The role of Title I

For students who are at risk and meet certain economic qualifications, Title I is another program that can help address their needs. Specifically, Title I is a federal program designed to give educational assistance to students living in areas of poverty. It is one of the oldest and largest federal programs supporting elementary and secondary education, and more than 90 percent of the school systems in the United States receive some sort of Title I funding (U.S. Department of Education, 2015a). The Title I program provides financial assistance to public schools with high numbers or percentages of students who are poor to help ensure that all students can achieve state standards.

Eligibility for Title I is based on the number of students in your school who receive free or reduced lunches and by the number of students in the district who are living in poverty (U.S. Department of Education, 2015a). Title I funds may be used for students from preschool to high school age. Funds are used to hire staff, purchase materials, and provide supports for students identified as low achieving in reading and math. Title I services can be provided either as targeted assistance or as schoolwide assistance. Under targeted assistance, specific students would qualify for Title I services; under schoolwide assistance, funds can be used to assist all students.

Summary

As a general education teacher, you have many kinds of students, including those with disabilities who do not qualify for special education services but do qualify for a plan under Section 504, a nondiscrimination law that protects students with such disabilities as ADD/ADHD, allergies, eating disorders, and past drug addiction, among others. A Section 504 plan is usually much briefer than an IEP, but it typically specifies the aids, services, and accommodations a student will require. Policies and personnel involved in developing the plan vary from district to district. Both students who are gifted and talented and those who are at risk also deserve attention in the classroom. Some of these students may become eligible for special education and related services; however, many will not. Recommended practices for gifted and talented students include curriculum compacting, curriculum acceleration, and enrichment activities. Students who are at risk will benefit from individualized attention to their specific situation, setting reasonable expectations, involving other school personnel who can provide needed resources, and working closely with family members.

All of these students are entitled to receive an education that will help them benefit from their educational program, and most likely it will be the general education teacher who will provide most (if not all) of that education.

6

Transition

In this chapter we discuss transition—its definition and components—with a focus on the role of the general education classroom teacher. We include specific recommendations for elementary and secondary education teachers and what they can do to help students with disabilities get ready for postschool life. The chapter also covers recommendations for working with preschool students as they are transitioning from early childhood special education to K–12 special education.

Skills to Teach for Transition—and Life

The skills discussed in this section are generally thought of as incidental skills gained through experience. As teachers know, however, many students benefit from explicit instruction in these "life skills," and students with disabilities may benefit particularly. We believe teaching these skills—all of which foster independence in school and beyond it—should be part of the curriculum from preschool through high school. Some of these will need to be retaught many times over a student's career.

Arriving on time. Beginning in elementary school and continuing as temporal awareness and executive functions develop, students need to be made aware of the importance of showing up on time for classes, activities, and events. They should learn and practice strategies that will help them do so, such as planning ahead by determining how long it will take to get ready and budgeting for travel time. General education teachers in elementary and middle school should hold students accountable (to the best of the students' ability) for showing up on time and make sure they understand the consequences of not being in a place at the appointed time.

Asking for help. All students need to know who they would go to for help if they have issues, concerns, or questions, and to realize that it is

OK to stop what they are doing to ask for help. It is important to foster independence, but we also want students to know there will be times when they should stop what they are doing and seek assistance. Not only will they need to understand when it is appropriate to do so, but they will also need to know how to appropriately ask and who to ask—all of which depend on the specific tasks and activities at hand. You can use a variety of activities to start their thinking about the process of when to ask for help. As a future work skill, this is invaluable.

Listening to directions. Being able to listen to directions will have a dramatic effect on a student's independence and success, both in school and in adult life. This is a skill all teachers should target and work to develop in students. Not hearing or mishearing directions is a big problem for many students and can cause complications and difficulties in many different areas.

Working independently. The main goal and purpose of special education is to help students become as independent as possible, in both school and work. It is important to address independent-living skills as appropriate, based on students' level of need. Although they will likely have to work with others, students must also be able to work alone. This skill is closely aligned with some of the other skills, most notably knowing when to ask for help.

Paying attention to others. Although it is important to teach students to work independently, teachers should also underscore the value of being aware of what is going on around them and seeing if what they are doing is the same as or different from what their peers are doing. Students need to recognize this difference and be able to either ask for help or adjust themselves to the group norm. This skill can help rectify a problem before it becomes severe.

IMPORTANT POINTS

- Transition is not just for students with disabilities, though their needs may require that they receive more attention than other students.

- Teachers should not wait until students are 16 or older to discuss postschool matters.

- Transition includes making parents aware of resources and activities that can help as their child goes through various stages in postschool life.

- Schools have a responsibility to help a student prepare for postschool life, and all the student's teachers should work together in this effort.

- Transitioning from early childhood special education services to K–12 special education services and from elementary to secondary schooling can be difficult for some students and their parents, and helping them through the process is an important school function.

Handling frustration. Students need to learn and understand that everything will not always go their way, and sometimes they will get frustrated by the course of events and the problems presented. We need to make sure we help students understand that frustration is a very real human emotion, that we all have to deal with it, and that there are appropriate ways of doing so.

Developing social skills. As educators, we are continually addressing social skills with students, and instruction in these skills will probably need to be repeated multiple times. It is important to teach students how to recognize and deal with problems or issues related to interacting with others. Sometimes the rules are not clear and will vary depending on the situation. Some of the social skills that students typically struggle with are those related to personal space, greetings, reciprocal play, conversation, perspective taking, and negotiating.

Understanding empathy. Some of the individuals students interact with will have issues affecting their feelings and performance. We need to make sure students learn skills related to showing compassion, including understanding the difference between appropriate and inappropriate comments.

Promoting self-determination. Students with disabilities have feelings, attitudes, and preferences about their future and about their daily activities. We need to give them an opportunity to voice their interests and concerns, but they also need to understand that just because they make a choice does not mean it will automatically occur; other issues and concerns also come into play. For instance, a student's desire for a specific food for every meal is unlikely to be fulfilled, for either logistical or health reasons. It is important to honor requests when possible and provide students an opportunity to make choices—and then, in turn, to learn from the choices they have made.

Transitioning from Preschool to Elementary School

For some students with disabilities, the transition from preschool to school-age services is a considerable challenge. Typically, the students who receive special education services in preschool are those with more severe or noticeable disabilities. Some have been receiving services for a few years, and they are about to enter K–12 schooling, where the rules, settings, and expectations are different. This section describes the typical preschool program for students with disabilities; identifies some of the aspects of transition for these students that should be addressed, highlighting the differences between preschool and school-age services; and lists specific steps that you, as a general education teacher, can take to help facilitate the transition for both the student and the parents.

Preschool special education services

Preschool special education services are available for students ages 3 to 5 who have disabilities or developmental delays affecting their ability to learn. Just like services for school-age students, these services are provided to eligible students free of charge. Special education services can help to address concerns regarding the preschool student's learning, speech, physical development, behavior, or other areas. The qualifications for students ages 3 to 5 are the same as those for school-age students, with the exception of one additional disability category: developmental delay.

Students eligible for special education services starting at age 3 receive an IEP; however, students with a disability who get services before age 3 get an IFSP, or individualized family services plan. Similar to an IEP, an IFSP is a plan that details a student's strengths and needs and states how an agency will meet the student's and the family's unique needs. Because its primary focus is on the student and the family, it includes family objectives as well as student goals. Services and settings may vary from one location to another. Services may be provided at home, at a preschool or student-care center, in a special education setting, or in a combination of any of these settings. For example, some students may receive physical therapy to address problems with mobility, whereas others may work with a speech language pathologist on articulation disorders or language delays. Some students with more significant needs may attend small, structured special education preschool classes.

Transitioning between school settings

The transition out of preschool services likely means that the location of the services will switch from a small setting with few students to a larger setting—typically an elementary school. Teachers need to work with the student and the parents to help them make the transition to the new setting, explaining the rules and requirements and informing them about whom to contact with questions. The following list of suggestions is intended to help students and parents make the transition between school settings. They are appropriate for transition from preschool to elementary, and also from elementary to middle school and to high school. Not every one of these may be necessary, but they suggest what can be done to help the student and the parent with the transition process.

• Set up a meeting to introduce yourself to the child and the parents. The meeting can take place in the classroom to show the student and the parent the new location of their educational experience. This can help to reduce anxiety and allow both to become more comfortable with the location.

• Allow the student to play on the playground, walk around the school, and see the classroom, if the meeting did not take place there.

• Discuss the rules and expectations for the new setting.

• Allow the parents an opportunity to share specific concerns they may have about their child, such as food allergies, issues related to toileting, or the need for frequent ingestion of calories.

• Ask the parents about the services they received in the previous setting and the specifics of what the student was provided. For example, if the student received speech and language instruction, ask for specifics that can be reinforced or addressed in the classroom setting.

• Provide the parents the name of a special education contact person who will be available to answer questions.

• Introduce the student and the parent to the principal, the school secretary, the school nurse, and the school counselor. Doing so can provide the family with reassurance that people will be available to work with and for the student.

• During the first week, send notices home to let the family know how things are going.

• Allow the parent to volunteer in the classroom after a few weeks to let them see the other students and how their child interacts with others.

• Keep the special education staff, and the principal, apprised as to how the student is functioning in the new setting.

• Be willing to attend meetings to discuss how the student is doing.

• Answer parents' e-mails and calls promptly. Be careful not to get into an endless loop with questions, but allow time for the parents to make the transition.

• Assign the student a peer buddy. This practice can help all students as they are making their way in a new educational setting.

As with any student who comes to school for the first time, do not expect things to start out perfectly. There will be problems, and you may need to talk with the parents about how the student is, or is not, adjusting.

Postsecondary Transition

The purpose of postsecondary transition is to help students and their families prepare for life after high school, which can be a major concern for students receiving special education. Transition is intended to be a coordinated set of activities provided by the school and outside agencies, and it is designed to promote a successful shift to postsecondary education, employment, and/or independent living. These activities are outlined in the student's IEP and should focus on the ability and interests of the students, and not on what they cannot do (Flexer, Baer, Luft, & Simmons, 2007).

The federal regulations in IDEA that relate to secondary transition include the following formal definition of "transition services":

Transition services means a coordinated set of activities for a child with a disability that—

- Is designed to be within a results-oriented process, that is focused on improving the academic and functional achievement of the child with a disability to facilitate the child's movement from school to postschool activities, including postsecondary education, vocational education, integrated employment (including supported employment), continuing and adult education, adult services, independent living, or community participation;
- Is based on the individual child's needs, taking into account the child's strengths, preferences, and interests; and
- Includes instruction, related services, community experiences, the development of employment and other post-school adult living objectives, and, if appropriate, acquisition of daily living skills and provision of a functional vocational evaluation. [34 CFR 300.43 (a)]; [20 U.S.C. 1401(34)]

Figure 6.1 shows a sample statement of transition services.

In its reauthorization of IDEA in 2004, the U.S. Congress recognized that students with disabilities needed more assistance to help them get ready for postschool life (Kochhar-Bryant, 2008). Congress expressly stated they would like schools to require more and better transition planning (Flexer et al., 2007). As the definition indicates, the goal of transition is to promote successful outcomes for students with disabilities to either postschool education or employment. In turn, measuring students' success in moving to postsecondary institutions or employment would become an important component of accountability for schools (Kochhar-Bryant, 2008).

Figure 6.1 / Sample Statement of Transition Services Needed to Meet Postsecondary Goals

STATEMENT OF TRANSITION SERVICES NEEDED

Each area must be considered by the IEP team. After consideration, only areas determined necessary to meet the individual needs of the student must be addressed.

Transition Service Area	Transition Services Needed to Assist the Student in Meeting Postsecondary Goals (Include Time Line for Achievement)	Person or Agency Responsible	Discussed, Not Needed
Instruction	J will demonstrate personal safety (stranger danger, sexually transmitted diseases, pregnancy prevention, consumer safety, etc.) by the time he graduates from high school.	student, family, school staff, Altacare	
Employment	J will learn and use effective communication skills (staying on topic during conversations, maintaining focus, not interrupting, choosing conversation topics, etc.) by the end of his senior year of high school.	student, family, school staff, Altacare	
Community Experiences	J will participate in a variety of community events (e.g., sporting events, craft shows, concerts, church events) each year of high school.	student, family	
Postschool Adult Living	J will meet with a vocational rehabilitation (VR) counselor before his senior year of high school.	student, school staff, VR, family	
Related Services	J's family will explore legal status with regard to decision making before J reaches the age of majority.	parent	
Daily Living Skills (If Appropriate)	J will take cooking/life skills classes and practice cooking, shopping, and housekeeping skills during each year of high school.	student, family, school staff	
Functional Vocational Assessment	Arrange functional vocational assessment before graduating high school if the student qualifies for VR or developmental disabilities (DD) services.	student, VR or DD services, family	

When does postschool transition planning begin?

Postschool transition planning is required to begin at age 16 (or age 14, in some states), but for most students, age 16 is too late. Because developing a plan for a student's transition is part of the IEP team's responsibilities, the process can begin before age 16.

Why should it begin earlier? Depending on the severity of the disability and the student's and family's goals for the future, specific issues need to be discussed and addressed well before the student turns 16. Many of the skills necessary for independent living and functioning need to be taught early on—and repeatedly, beginning in elementary school. Additionally, many younger students have interests and aspirations regarding the kind of work they would like to do. They can start exploring activities relating to those jobs at a young age and gather information that will help them make informed decisions when they get older.

What is included in transition planning?

Although transition planning is an individualized process, there are some commonalities. Specifically, the federal regulations state the following:

> Beginning not later than the first IEP to be in effect when the child turns 16, or younger if determined appropriate by the IEP Team, and updated annually thereafter, the IEP must include—
>
> (1) Appropriate measurable postsecondary goals based upon age appropriate transition assessments related to training, education, employment and, where appropriate, independent living skills; and
>
> (2) The transition services (including courses of study) needed to assist the child in reaching those goals [§300.320(b)].

Transition plans vary based on the student's individual needs, interests, strengths, and preferences. The IEP team should meet to talk about these aspects of the student's life and future goals to ensure that all team members are working toward the same end. The team should make sure the specific goals and objectives of the IEP relate to helping the student prepare for postschool life. For example, if a student with a learning disability wants to go to college, the student's high school experience should include developing skills that are important for success in college, such as writing, time management, note taking, and perhaps specific skills related to a possible major. A student with a disability who does not intend to go to college but is interested in auto mechanics could be provided with opportunities to shadow someone who works on cars and with help in determining the specific skills necessary for that line of work. Courses and experiences during the transition period should ensure that the student graduates with the skills needed for success in the next step after high school, whether that is continued education, a vocation, or independent living (see Figure 6.2 for a sample course of study).

Figure 6.2 / Sample Course of Study for Transition Planning

COURSE OF STUDY

Describe below a course of study designed within a results-oriented process to (1) focus on improving the academic and functional achievement of the student; (2) directly relate to the student's measurable postsecondary goals and the student's strengths, preferences, and interests; and (3) promote movement from school to postschool settings and activities.

Anticipated Graduation Date: 2020

Credits earned to date: 0

Total credits needed for graduation: 21

School Year 2016–17	Credit	School Year 2017–18	Credit
English 1	1	English II	1
Basic Math	1	Life Skills Math	1
World History	1	Physical Science	1
Altacare		Ceramics	1
Health/PE	0.5	Health/PE	0.5
Study Skills	1	Study Skills	1
Foods 1	1	Foods 2	1

Total number of credits: 12.00

Obvious sources for information related to the transition plan are conversations with the student and the parents, as well as the student's general education teachers. Interest inventories and specific skills assessments can help students make decisions about possible future career choices; school counselors or special education teachers typically administer these (Figure 6.3 shows a sample feedback report, including results of a student's assessments). One thing to keep in mind is the need to help students be realistic in their goals. For example, despite the number of students who participate in high school sports, few ever become professional athletes. Even if they excel at a particular sport, they need to be aware of more promising alternatives for a career. The same conversation applies to students who say, for example, that they want to run their own business but either lack an idea or seem to lack the motivation to do any work on their own. The goal is not to quash students' dreams, but to guide them through a decision-making process that results in achievable, measurable goals (see Figure 6.4).

Figure 6.3 / Sample Feedback Report on Transition Services

TRANSITION SERVICES

Student's Desired Postschool Activities *(in the areas of postsecondary education; vocational education; integrated employment, including supported employment; continuing and adult education; adult services; and independent living or community participation)*

J says that he would like to study art at North Idaho College in Coeur d'Alene. He would like to eventually live in Loma, Missouri. However, his interests and plans vary considerably from day to day. This variability is evident on his transition assessments as well.

Results of Age-Appropriate Transition Assessments (results attached)

Training:

In October 2015, J completed the Missouri Career Information System (MCIS) O*NET interest profiler. His highest scores (13) were in the areas of Enterprising (work activities related to starting up and carrying out projects, especially business ventures, with a preference for action rather than thought) and Investigative (work activities focused on thinking more than on physical activity). He scored 12 in Conventional Interests (activities that follow set procedures and routines) and 0 in Social Interests (activities that deal with communication and working with others). J has not had a job or received any kind of specialized training to date.

Education:

J's midterm grades included 5 *B*s and 1 *A* in his core classes. On J's most recent Woodcock Johnson III Normative Update Tests of Achievement, he scored in the 14th percentile (low average) in Broad Reading, 8th percentile (borderline) in Broad Math, and in the 13th percentile (low average) in Broad Written Language. His highest score was in the 30th percentile (average) in Oral Language. His lowest score was in Academic Applications at the 7th percentile (borderline).

Employment:

J took the Reading-Free Vocational Interest Inventory in October 2015. His responses showed an above-average interest in the areas of Clerical (general office work such as running errands, sorting and delivering letters, furnishing workers with supplies, and routine office tasks); Food Service (preparation and serving of food); and Materials Handling (warehousing, loading, unloading, sorting, stacking, hauling and delivering merchandise). J's highest career cluster (82nd percentile for his age) was in Food Service-Handling Operations.

Independent Living Skills (if appropriate):

In October 2015, J took the Ansell-Casey Life Skills Assessment (ACLSA) Youth 2 Inventory. His scores were as follows: Communication—raw score, 67%, mastery score, 22%; Daily Living—raw 48%, mastery 8%; Self-Care—raw 46%, mastery 0%; Social Relationships— raw 67%, mastery 43%; Work and Study Skills—raw 67%, mastery 27%. The discrepancy between raw and mastery scores indicates that J believes he does well in these areas but his responses do not show mastery. For example, J indicated that he does not know how to save money, does not purchase items independently, cannot fix meals on his own, does not know how to prevent pregnancy, etc.

Figure 6.4 / Sample of a Statement of Measurable Postsecondary Goals

---

MEASURABLE POSTSECONDARY GOALS

Measurable postsecondary goals are based on age-appropriate transition assessments related to training, education, employment, and, if appropriate, independent living skills. Clearly specify the desired level of achievement.

Measurable Postsecondary Goal(s)—Education or Training:

Within a year of graduating from high school, J will be studying art at North Idaho College in Coeur d'Alene, Idaho.

Measurable Postsecondary Goal(s)—Employment:

Within five years of graduating from high school, J will be employed in a job in Loma, Missouri, that incorporates his art interests.

Measurable Postsecondary Goal(s)—Independent Living Skills (if appropriate):

Within a year of graduating from high school, J will be living in a dorm or with a roommate in Coeur d'Alene, Idaho.

Who should participate in transition planning?

Transition planning for students with disabilities is an integral responsibility of the IEP team, and all team members should participate in developing the plan, including the student. Students are often not included in developing their IEPs in elementary school, but as transition planning begins, they should be involved as much as possible. Team members need to ask students to share their preferences and should pay close attention to their answers, realizing that these responses may change over time. This approach to transition planning—putting the student at the center of the process—is what is known as person-centered planning.

Parents should also be heavily involved. The IDEA amendments related to transition originated from the realization that many students were graduating from high school without having been taught independent-living and work-related skills, leaving parents to attempt to help their children navigate a system of services that are very different from those offered through K–12 education. It is important to remember that parents may be the only source of support for many of these students after high school, and their viewpoints are a key element in the decision-making process.

Finally, schools are responsible for inviting representatives from other agencies (such as rehabilitative services agencies and postsecondary education institutions) and vocational rehabilitation counselors to be part of the transition planning process, as needed. Such agencies could also be responsible for the delivery of some of the services needed by the student.

Summary

Transition is a normal part of every person's life, and the goal for school-related transitions is to make the process as smooth as possible for the student and the family. Schools are responsible to help ease this path for students, especially those with disabilities. Parents will need to familiarize themselves with the law, the rights of their child, and the school's particular procedures. Schools can help by providing clear information (in multiple languages, if necessary) online and in print, and by making it easy for parents to contact the relevant staff (such as the school psychologist). Starting this process before the start of school and with the goal of ongoing home-school collaboration is important for successful transitions.

7

Classroom Management and Student Behavior

Student behavior can be challenging and can require a lot of a teacher's time and attention. All students, whether they have disabilities or are typically developing, are to be held accountable to the same school code. However, for your students with disabilities, you will need to follow different rules regarding suspension and be mindful of behavioral plans, functional behavioral assessments, and behavior rating scales. In this chapter we highlight these components and discuss what you need to know about working with students with disabilities when it comes to classroom management and student behavior.

Teaching Students Desired Behaviors

As a classroom teacher, you likely will be able to teach a student vowel sounds, math facts, or how to diagram a sentence. These academic tasks are critical to a student's success, and versions of these skills are included in the summative grades included on report cards. Seldom specified in what teachers are required to teach are the behaviors necessary for classroom success, including following directions, knowing when to ask for help, knowing where to go for help, and getting along with others. To effectively participate in your class, students—whether they have a disability or not—need to be directly taught the behaviors you expect to see. If you want students to turn in their papers in one location, teach them to do so. If you want them to use only one side of the paper, teach this, along with all the other classroom behaviors you expect.

Underlying reasons for behavior

Before we discuss working with students who have behavior problems, it is important to consider why these problems may exist.

Behavior as communication. It may seem on some days that students are intentionally trying to cause problems. They may indeed be using behavior as communication—attempting to tell you that an assigned task is difficult, that they do not understand, that they are bored, that they feel uncomfortable, and so on. Before you take other steps, consider whether you might need to revise your instruction, making changes in how you present materials, how you articulate expectations, and how you reinforce behaviors.

Environmental factors. The environment may have a lot to do with what students are doing and how they are performing. You need to consider the classroom's lighting, the amount of visual and auditory distraction students are exposed to, how seating arrangement might factor in, and whether the classroom's materials and furniture are meeting the students' needs.

Learned response. Have students learned they can cause problems or make noises and not be held accountable for class work? Have their past teachers permitted them to opt out of classwork as long as they sit quietly in the back of the classroom? Getting answers to questions like these can guide you toward a better course of action.

Changing behavior

We guarantee that you will have some students whose behavior you will want to change, but changing a student's behavior is easier said than done.

IMPORTANT POINTS

- Students with disabilities can be disciplined for violating the school code just like typically developing students; however, different rules apply relating to the suspension and expulsion of students with disabilities.

- When addressing student behavior, the district must ensure students are continuing to receive services to allow them to make progress toward the goals and objectives in their IEPs.

- All acts of bullying must be taken seriously.

- Recording the number of times a student engages in negative acts is an integral part of the process for determining the level of support required by a student.

There will always be some factors outside your control. Focus instead on the ones you *can* control—the ones that address

- How you manage the classroom
- The classroom schedule
- How much work you assign
- The type of work you assign
- Deadlines for completion of work
- The rules you set
- How you enforce rules
- What students are expected to do during downtime

Another factor that you can control—and change—is the manner in which you set up the classroom, which can dramatically alter the students' experience. The following are important questions all teachers should ask themselves as a part of classroom setup:

- Is my classroom well organized?
- Can staff and students easily locate materials?
- Does the classroom setup facilitate smooth transitions?
- Can I reduce auditory and visual stimuli?
- Are boundaries clearly established for behaviors?
- Do students know where to go for certain activities or tasks?
- Do students know what to do when they finish an assignment?

Taking the time to consider how you can improve your classroom setup and clarify expected procedures can lead to better experiences for students —and for you.

Observing and Recording Behavior

Part of your work as a teacher is to identify the specific behaviors that are causing problems for the student and the class, and to what extent those behaviors are problematic. In addition, you need to determine the function, or payoff, of the behaviors, recognizing that students often engage in certain behaviors because they get something out it. To do all these things, you need to gather data, which is typically done by observing the behaviors and recording what you see.

Defining the behavior

Defining the problematic behavior is a crucial step. The definition should be specific enough so that anyone else observing the student can clearly see whether or not the behavior is occurring. The following is a list of terms that are often used to describe students with behavior problems:

- Weird
- Lazy
- Bad attitude
- Mean
- Disrespectful
- Causes problems
- Seems off

Your first thought might be that these terms are inappropriate because they are judgmental, and although this is true, the greater concern is that the terms are imprecise and do not help others understand the specifics of the student's problem. Contrast the above with the following list of terms, which provides more accurate—and more helpful—descriptors:

- Talks about subjects that are off topic
- Does not complete class assignments
- Lays head down on desk
- Argues when given a direction
- Touches other students
- Is late for school four out of every five days
- Talks with only two other students in the class
- Needs redirection from the teacher once every 20 minutes

As noted, it is important to clearly identify the specifics of the behavior. Yes, a student may be disrespectful, but what does that really mean? Does that mean the student does not make eye contact when walking down the hall? Does it mean the student does not say "excuse me" when bumping into another student? Does it mean the student takes items from other students without asking? Clarity is important to the initial part of this process.

Recording behaviors

Once you have defined a specific problematic behavior, you need to determine how you will record this behavior. Recording behaviors in a large class can be difficult, given all your other responsibilities, but it is an important part of determining the level, amount, or frequency of the behavior.

Behaviors can be recorded in various ways, but the goal is always to present the data in a consumable form, such as a graph. Here we describe different methods of recording behaviors. Determining which one to use depends on the specifics of the behavior and the needs of the student.

Rate and frequency recording. This method involves counting the number of times a behavior occurs in a specific period. This method is appropriate if the behavior can be easily counted and has a clear beginning and end; it is inappropriate for a behavior that is continual or extremely frequent, such as leg shaking or pencil tapping. Rate data should be used if the length of observation time varies from day to day—for example, if you record during differing time periods on Monday and Tuesday. Use frequency measures over a consistent length of time (20 minutes or a class period, for example) for comparisons over multiple days.

Duration recording. This approach documents how long a behavior persists by recording the time the behavior begins and the time that it ends. Use this method if you are concerned about how long the student's behavior is persisting or if the length of time of a specific behavior affects its severity. For example, you may want to know how long a student is in a tantrum, is crying, or is in the bathroom.

Interval recording. This method involves dividing your observation period into a number of smaller time periods, observing the student during the specific time period, and then recording whether the behavior occurred or not. Interval recording often takes less time and effort, especially if the behavior occurs at a high frequency, because the observer records the behavior only once during the time period. Interval recording only provides a rough estimate of the total number of times a behavior occurs. Do not make the intervals too long. The shorter the interval, the more accurate you will be.

Latency recording. This method is concerned with measuring the time that it takes for students to respond to something you ask them to do. For example, you might record how long it takes the student to comply with a request, put away materials, go sit at her desk, or begin an assignment.

Filling out behavior rating scales. Behavior rating scales come in various forms and are used to rate how the student's behavior compares to the behavior of others in the classroom and how the behavior changes over time. Talk with the special education teachers on your staff to find out which rating scales they like. Results from behavior rating scales are usually interpreted by the school psychologist or other specialists.

As a general education classroom teacher, you will probably be asked to administer a scale related to ADHD more than any other type. The request may come because a student is suspected of having ADHD, has been recently diagnosed with ADHD, or has been prescribed medication and the student's physician needs more information about progress.

The following are four of the most commonly administered rating scales, each of which comes with directions and suggestions for use:

- *Achenbach System of Empirically Based Assessment (ASEBA)*
  - Includes forms for parent, teacher, and student
  - Includes direct observation form and interview form
  - Rates student on positive behaviors and behavioral syndromes

- *Behavior Assessment System for Children, 2nd edition (BASC-2)*
  - Includes rating scales for parent and teacher to complete
  - Includes a developmental history form and a self-report form for students ages 8–25
  - Distinguishes between ADD, depression, other behavioral concerns, and social maladjustments

- *Behavior Rating Profile, 2nd edition (BRP-2)*
  - Includes forms for parent, teacher, and student
  - Allows for comparison among student, teacher, and parent perceptions of the student
  - Categorizes student's perceptions of school, home, and peer relationships
  - Evaluates student's feelings about school and relationships with peers and parents

- *Conners Comprehensive Behavior Rating Scales (CBRS)—Revised*
  - Multidimensional scales assess ADHD and other disorders that may coexist with attention disorders
  - Ties with DSM-IV diagnoses
  - Assesses various behavioral dimensions: oppositional, cognitive problems/inattention, hyperactivity, anxious-shy, perfectionism, social problems, psychosomatic

We want to note that student behaviors that affect others should also be recorded—both those that cause problems for other students and those that will help the student get along with others. Obviously, the behaviors that need to be changed are those that have a negative effect on the student's future.

Examining the data

No matter what data-gathering method you use, graphing the data is a critical next step. It's a practice that, over time, will clarify what is happening for you and for others, and support sound decision making. It will help parents and others understand the magnitude of a problem and whether programmatic changes are necessary, or if there are certain strategies that work, or settings or times of days in which the behavior is better or worse.

When you examine behavioral data you have collected, there are several factors to keep in mind.

How the behavior compares with that of other students. Some students may seem to have more problems than others, but in reality, they just get caught more often.

The context of the behavior. For example, noisy or active behaviors may be acceptable on the playground but inappropriate in the classroom. Similarly, running across a classroom would be deemed inappropriate behavior in most instances, but if a student runs in response to a loud noise or a large insect, the behavior would be understandable, even expected. When considering the context of behavior, also consider what happened both immediately before the behavior and immediately after it. This is called an A-B-C analysis—Antecedent, Behavior, and Consequence. The chart in Figure 7.1 is a sample of a form you might use for an A-B-C analysis.

Figure 7.1 / Sample A–B–C Observation Form

Student: _____ Setting: _____

Observer: _____

Date	Time	Duration of the behavior	What happened before the behavior?	Describe the behavior	What was the consequence of the behavior?
3/30/16	9:23	27 min.	The teacher asked the student to write a five-sentence paragraph and gave him a sheet of lined paper.	Student climbed under the table and refused to come out. Verbal and visual cues were used to coax the student out.	The student did not have to complete the writing assignment. He came out after the class left for PE.

The purpose of using the A-B-C chart is to see if there are consistent triggers or settings in which the behavior occurs. This type of data is very helpful but also a bit labor intensive to gather and report. Often the school psychologist or the special education teacher will help you set up a system to collect the data, as well as assist with the interpretation. Not all A-B-C analyses need to record negative behaviors; you can use the same analysis to record when positive behaviors occur in the classroom and then reinforce those behaviors. In addition, you can observe what the student finds reinforcing and use that to shape correct behavior in the future.

Rules for Disciplining Students with Disabilities

Students with disabilities—both those eligible for special education and those with a Section 504 plan—can be disciplined for violation of school rules. However, different rules apply for students with disabilities in regard to suspension and expulsion.

First, students with disabilities can be suspended from school, but not for more than 10 days in an academic year. Once a student has been suspended for 10 days, the 11th day is considered a change of placement, and the school district cannot unilaterally change a student's placement. Therefore, a manifestation determination meeting must be held to determine if the behavior that caused the student to be suspended is due either to the disability or to the IEP not being implemented. Once the IEP team makes that determination, the next steps in the student's education can proceed, and the IEP can be adjusted as needed. If the behavior is determined to be not the result of the student's disability or nonimplementation of the IEP, the student is eligible only for the services in the IEP, not the entirety of his education.

Second, the school may call the police if the student brings a weapon or drugs to school. After all, a school is responsible for ensuring a safe environment for all students. However, after calling the police, the school must follow a discipline policy that reflects the process just described.

Third, students with disabilities cannot be expelled—even if they bring a weapon to school. However, even though they are still entitled to receive an education, it does not necessarily have to be in the same setting where they were previously. For example, they could be sent to an interim alternative education setting after a behavioral incident. It is important to be knowledgeable about your school's policy regarding a student bringing a weapon or drugs to school, which may include the district's right to make a unilateral placement decision for up to 45 days. (The number of days may differ depending on your state regulations. Check to see what is legal in your state.)

Fourth, if a student engages in behaviors that are deemed harmful to the student or to others, the district should develop a plan to work with the student that includes goals and objectives in the IEP. The district should also consider developing a behavior intervention plan.

Fifth, if a student has been suspended frequently, the district should hold an IEP meeting to develop a program for the student and possibly alter the supports provided. It is the district's responsibility to request this meeting and develop a plan. As with other students with disabilities, it is the district's responsibility to ensure that changes are made to help students whose behavior is not improving. This is especially true if a student is having frequent outbursts and is therefore unable to make progress in the classroom.

PBIS and FBA: Frameworks for Addressing Behavior Challenges

There are many ways to address a student's behavior challenges, but two of the most common approaches are Positive Behavioral Interventions and Supports (PBIS) and functional behavioral assessment (FBA). Together, they can help you deal with the issues you can control. Dealing with discipline or behavioral problems is necessary to help ensure that all students can receive instruction and are not overly distracted by problems. Understanding PBIS and FBA will help you prevent, identify, and then address behavior problems. You can also expect to work closely with special education teachers on the development of appropriate behavior management strategies.

Positive Behavioral Interventions and Supports

PBIS is a framework for working with all students, not just those with disabilities. This point is worth noting because not all students with behavioral problems are eligible for special education, but they may need supports nevertheless.

Similar to the Response to Intervention (RTI) model that we discussed in Chapter 2, PBIS interventions are described based on their intensity, from least to most:

• *First Level*—These are schoolwide, or primary, interventions intended to help with school and classroom behaviors. This is where we teach all the students in the school the rules for conduct and appropriate behavior.

• *Second Level*—These are secondary interventions designed to prevent problems from becoming more serious. Examples of these can be small-group instruction or a social skills club.

• *Third Level*—Often called tertiary interventions, these are for students who have chronic or serious behavior problems. A student may receive a functional behavior assessment, and then possibly a behavior intervention plan.

PBIS has four main elements: (1) clearly defined outcomes, (2) a basis in behavioral and biomedical science, (3) practices demonstrated through research to be effective, and (4) a systematic approach that enhances the learning experience. For more information, please see www.pbis.org.

Functional behavioral assessment

When classroom interventions are not being effective and a student's behavior seems to be getting worse, the multidisciplinary team could consider a functional behavioral assessment, or FBA. The FBA is an approach that goes beyond what the behavior looks like to focus on identifying the factors that initiate, sustain, or end the behavior in question. (The A-B-C analysis described earlier in this chapter is one tool that may be used when completing an FBA.) The FBA zeroes in on why a student is displaying an undesired behavior, rather than just the behavior itself (Shea & Bauer, 2011). It seeks to identify the function or purpose of the behavior so that the team can develop a plan that allows the student to use another behavior to achieve the same, desired function. Figure 7.2 shows the components of a typical FBA.

The school psychologist or other special education staff person often facilitates the development of a functional behavioral assessment; however, most team members will have a role in the assessment. As the general education teacher, you would most likely be asked to answer questions regarding the student's behavior and strategies used in the classroom, and the effectiveness of those strategies. Here are some examples of typical questions:

• Does the student understand what to do in this situation?
• Does the student know he or she is engaging in unacceptable behavior?
• Can the student control the behavior?
• Does the student have the necessary skills to perform the desired behavior?

Figure 7.2 / Components of a Functional Behavioral Assessment (FBA)

- *Background Information*—Medical, mental health, educational, family, developmental

- *Target Behaviors*—Specific definitions, including intensity, frequency, duration, and educational impact for student, peers, and staff

- *Parent Input Regarding Target Behaviors and Strategies*—Parents' perspective on behavior triggers, strategies/consequences and their effect, self-calming techniques, motivators/reinforcers

- *Student Input Regarding Target Behaviors and Strategies*—Student's perspective on behavior triggers, strategies/consequences and their effect, self-calming techniques, motivators/reinforcers

- *Antecedents/Triggers*—Setting, tasks, and other possible contributing factors

- *Student Response to Consequences*—Actual and current consequences of behavior and the impact on the student, peers, and staff

- *Hypothesized Functions of Behavior*—What the student is seeking or obtaining as a result of the behavior

- *Possible Replacement Behaviors/Skills to Be Taught*—More appropriate/desired behaviors that will achieve the same function as the target behaviors

- *Preferred Reinforcers*—Items (including food), activities, and events the student finds reinforcing

---

Answering these questions can help determine if a student's behavior is the result of a skill deficit. If that is the case, the student needs to be taught the appropriate skill for the situation.

If the student has the skill to behave appropriately but for some reason continues not to do so, then he may not understand the rules or expectations. The following questions should help you identify whether the student has a disability or needs additional instruction in classroom skills or both:

- Is the student uncertain about the appropriateness of the behavior?
- Is the negative behavior rewarding?
- Does the behavior occur only in certain environments?
- Is the student trying to get out of doing another task?
- What rule is the student breaking?

Developing a Behavior Plan

After completing an FBA and determining the function of the behavior, the next step is to develop a behavior plan for the student. This is typically done by a team. Behavior plans can cover a range of issues, from what the student should do in specific situations to broad statements about such things as interacting with others on the playground. The behavior plan has to be tailored to the student and must help the student understand appropriate behaviors, with clear incentives to work toward specified rewards. Here are some tips for developing a behavior management plan:

1. Use the information from the FBA to determine the function the behavior is serving.

2. Describe the behavior in specific, observable terms.

3. Develop long-term goals for behavior, stating them in positive behavioral terms.

4. Write the plan down and go over it with the student and the parents.

5. Develop an expected time line for achievement.

6. Develop a list of alternative, acceptable behaviors. These behaviors should be taught and rewarded as replacements for the targeted problem behavior.

7. Ensure that the behavior plan includes enough detail to provide the student with a clear understanding of what is expected.

8. Explain the relationship of each goal to the student and the parents.

9. Address how others from the student's class will be included.

10. Include steps for rewards if the student improves faster than expected.

11. Identify who is responsible for ensuring implementation of the plan.

12. Review and revise the plan on a regular basis.

13. If the plan does not appear to be effective, review it and reconsider the function of the behaviors and the rewards.

Following up on the last tip, a behavior management plan should include a way to record the student's behavior so that you can see if the student is making progress and also to identify any areas that need additional attention. Figure 7.3 shows two examples of charts used to record behavior.

Dealing with Bullying

Most schools recognize bullying as the serious concern that it is and are addressing it in various ways. The definition of bullying specifically states that it is behavior that does harm and that is repeated over time. Bullying takes many forms and can cause problems for the education of all students, but especially students with disabilities, who may be having problems either academically or socially and who sometimes lack the communication skills to express what others are doing to them. Such students may be bullied or

Figure 7.3 / Sample Charts for Recording Student Behavior

Desired behavior ☺	Start of day to morning recess 8:20–10:00	Morning recess to lunch break 10:15–11:40	Lunch break to afternoon recess 12:30–2:00	Afternoon recess to end of day 2:15–3:10
Greeted peers and adults appropriately?	☺	☺	☺	☺
Was helpful with peers and adults?	☺	☺	☺	☺
Asked permission appropriately?	☺	☺	☺	☺
Entered and left classroom quietly?	☺	☺	☺	☺
Kept hands, feet, and objects to self?	☺	☺	☺	☺
Followed directions well?	☺	☺	☺	☺

Para or teacher: Mark each goal as either a 1 (successful) or a 0 (unsuccessful), depending on what [student's name] earns in your class.	Date_____						
	Period						
Goals	1	2	3	4	5	6	7
1. Prepared for class—Is on time for class, with assignment notebook, pen/pencil, textbook, homework, folder, clothes, etc. Is clean and ready for school.							
2. Stays in class area the entire time, without leaving for bathroom, drink, locker, etc.							
3. Follows directions the first time, without arguing or complaining.							
4. Participating in class—Works alone; asks for help if needed. Follows along and tries to answer discussion questions.							
5. Focused and engaged—Stays on task, with two or fewer reminders during class period.							
6. Integrity—Is honest and follows rules/procedures that have been taught.							
7. Responsibility—Fills out assignment book, gets teacher/ para initials, and picks up behavior sheet before leaving class.							
Teacher/Para Initials							

picked on more than others, and we need to ensure that they continue to receive the free appropriate public education they are entitled to, despite the actions of others.

If you think a student with a disability is being bullied, we suggest you take the following steps:

1. Do what is neccessary to ensure the student's immediate safety. This may require removing the student from the building.

2. Report the bullying to building-level administrators.

3. Report the bullying to the IEP team members.

4. Work with the IEP team to determine the impact the bullying may have on the disability. This could be an academic or social impact.

5. Work with the IEP team to make sure the student is receiving the required educational services and is making progress. The team may need to consider what skills need to be taught and could be included in the IEP to help the student deal with the bullying.

6. Provide opportunities for the student to meet with the school counselor.

7. Determine if a reevaluation is necessary. Does the student need additional assessments to determine if additional services are need?

8. Determine what additional information is necessary to help the student. Ask the parents for any information they may think is important.

9. Consider whether additional supervision could be provided.

10. Consider whether a change of placement or location is necessary, and make sure parents are informed about any proposed change.

11. Make sure the student continues to receive services in the least restrictive environment.

12. Make sure the student does not continue to be victimized.

13. Make sure the parents are informed about what is going on in school.

14. Keep others informed about changes to the student's schedule.

15. Make sure the other staff are aware of the bullying, and seek their help in monitoring and supporting the student.

16. Take action against the perpetrators.

Remember that your overarching goal is to make sure that all students feel safe in your classroom and school. Investigate all complaints, and do not wait for additional problems to appear. Be proactive in countering bullying.

Motivation Issues

Dealing with students who lack motivation can be one of the most frustrating aspects of a teacher's day-to-day responsibilities. Students with a lot of ability, both intellectually and socially, may demonstrate little desire to do academic work. Conversely, students with less ability may have a great desire to not only do the work, but to engage with more challenging material. As a teacher, it is only natural to want to spend more time with motivated students, so it is in your own interest to help keep all students interested and engaged in classroom activities. It is often difficult to determine if a student is not performing because of a lack of motivation or if the performance deficits are an aspect of the disability. Here are some tips for dealing with motivational issues:

• Look at the student's memory and processing speed scores and how these relate to the student's intellectual ability. Many times, deficits in these two areas will appear as a lack of motivation.

• Make sure the student is getting enough to eat, is sleeping, and has no other physical needs that are unmet. Talk with other staff and then the parents to make this determination.

• Work to involve the student in the lesson and make the material relevant to the student's life and interests.

• Try varying the classroom routine to create anticipation related to what the next activity will be.

• Provide opportunities for success, allowing the student to experience the boost of having learned or mastered a skill.

• Reward appropriate behavior by the student.

• If the student likes to be in charge of a class activity, provide that opportunity as a reinforcement.

• Talk with the student about individual goals.

• Make sure you and other teachers do not always focus on what the student does wrong or poorly. Emphasize the positive.

• Demonstrate by your own behavior that you want to be in the classroom, teaching your students.

Summary

When dealing with behavior problems, it is important to first consider possible underlying reasons and to focus on things that you can change, such as classroom management strategies and the type of work you ask students to do. Clearly defining problematic behavior is an important next step, followed by observing and recording instances in which the targeted behavior does—or does not—occur. It is essential to be aware of the various rules that apply to disciplining students with disabilities, such as the fact that they can be suspended from school, but not for more than 10 days in an academic year without additional steps and considerations.

Two frameworks for addressing challenging student behavior are Positive Behavioral Interventions and Supports (PBIS) and functional behavioral assessment (FBA). PBIS includes three levels of interventions intended to improve behavior, and FBAs involve an analysis of why a student is behaving in a particular way, so that the IEP team can develop an appropriate behavior plan.

Among the other issues that affect behavior, two of the most significant are bullying and lack of motivation. Addressing these can contribute to improved behavior and a better learning environment for all students.

8

Service Delivery Options, Related Services, and Other Service Providers

In this chapter we discuss the many different ways students with disabilities can receive special education services, the various settings where those services may be provided, and the other service providers who may be involved. In addition to classroom teachers, many other professionals work with students with disabilities, and they are all part of the team working to make sure students can make progress in school. As the general education teacher, you will work with these people and provide them with important information about how the student is doing in your classroom.

The Continuum of Services

As we noted in Chapter 1, the laws and regulations related to the education of students with disabilities require that they receive their education in the "least restrictive environment." This means the school district is to provide an education addressing the individual needs of the student in a setting that is as similar to the general education classroom as possible while still allowing the student to make progress in the curriculum. Only if the school cannot meet the needs of the student in the general education classroom can the student be moved to a more restrictive educational environment (Yell, 2015).

Some students have disabilities that require services that cannot be provided in the general education classroom. The IEP team is responsible for making decisions about the types and extent of services a student should receive, and where those services should be provided. The term used for the range of placements that must be available is called the "continuum of services." The student's placement on the continuum of services can change at any time to address the student's needs and must adhere to the "least restrictive environment" requirement. Here are some examples of decisions that *ignore* this requirement.

 • *Placing the student in a special education classroom based solely on the kind of disability the student has.* Although students identified with specific disabilities may share some common characteristics, placement in the same class or location may not be appropriate. The decision about the type and amount of services a student is to receive needs to be an individual decision made by the IEP team.

 • *Not trying different settings.* You cannot assume a student with a disability will not make progress in a certain setting without attempting to provide an education in that setting. As the team works to help the student succeed in the chosen setting, collect data to support the placement decision—including data on the efforts made to include the student with a disability and the results of those efforts. Only if it is clear that the setting is not meeting the student's needs should the IEP team consider changes to the student's placement.

 • *Not gathering data.* Repeatedly in this book we have stressed the importance of gathering data to make informed programmatic decisions about students with disabilities. You should use data to help make informed decisions not only about placement, as discussed in the previous paragraph, but also about the need for services and behavior management plans.

Service Delivery Options

Often when teachers think of special education, they think of a separate special education class.

IMPORTANT POINTS

- With appropriate supports, most students with disabilities can succeed in the general education classroom; some students, however, may need supports that are more intensive than what can be provided in a general education classroom.

- There are many ways to help students receive special education supports in the general education classroom.

- It is important for teachers to work closely with paraprofessionals, who provide important assistance for students with disabilities.

- Many students who qualify for special education services receive related services that are necessary to help them benefit from special education services.

- Sometimes general education teachers work with outside service providers to address student needs.

An important point to remember is that special education is a *service*, not a place. Many students receive most (if not all) of their special education services in the general education classroom. In this section we describe the different ways special education can be provided. Not all are appropriate for every student, and the team may identify additional options as they explore what is available in their building. Additionally, different approaches to working with a student can be combined, as certain ones may be more appropriate for a given activity.

Consultation, collaboration, and coteaching

Providing an education for eligible students often involves *consultation* and *collaboration,* which are two different things. Understanding these terms and the various methods they are part of will help you and the IEP team make sound placement decisions and provide appropriate services. In *consultation*, the special education teacher assists the general education teacher in making changes in the classroom or the way instruction is provided or material is presented; the general education teacher delivers all of the instruction. In *collaboration,* the general and special education teachers work together, and each has a different role in providing instruction, but the programs fit together well and work toward the same goal.

Coteaching is a collaborative approach to instruction in which two teachers, often a general education teacher and a special education teacher, work together to plan and then implement instruction for a class that includes students with disabilities. This can benefit not only the students with disabilities, but all students who are having difficulty with or are misunderstanding an assignment.

Coteaching requires time and energy, with both teachers committed to planning and delivering instruction together. It cannot be interpreted to mean one person teaches and the other works basically as a paraprofessional. And, although coteaching always involves an equal partnership in the planning and delivery of instruction, it can be implemented in several effective ways.

One teaches/one gathers data. In this model, one person takes the lead teaching role while the other observes and gathers data about the needs and progress of the designated students in the class to help plan future instruction. These roles can be switched to help deliver the instruction and share the responsibilities.

Station teaching. In station teaching, the lesson is divided equally between the two teachers, with each teaching half of the students in a small-group arrangement. The teachers need to work together to ensure the material is appropriately sequenced and the lessons build on each other. The teaching can be split according to teachers' strengths or interests. The class can be further divided, with a third group working independently or on seatwork.

Alternative teaching. This method is commonly used to provide instruction when there are four or five students with disabilities in the general education classroom. While one teacher works with a large group of students, the other teacher leads a small-group session targeting a specific skill or task. The one leading the small group may have to do multiple sessions with the students to ensure mastery. Alternatively, small groups can be set up as a class within a class, covering the standard material in greater depth and with a smaller student-to-teacher ratio.

One teaches/one assists. This method involves sharing instruction based on the teachers' strengths and interests. One teaches and the other circulates among the students and helps them as needed or assists those with problems and questions in the back of the room. To effectively cover the content, the teachers often reverse roles.

Push-in instruction

Increasingly, special education teachers are "pushing in" to the general education classroom, as opposed to "pulling out" students to work with them in a separate class. The descriptions in the previous section about coteaching also describe some of the common methods of push-in instruction. Here are some other points to keep in mind about push-in instruction:

• The teachers are equal partners in instruction. Make sure the students know this and are held accountable to both teachers.

• The special education teacher who is coming into the classroom needs to be provided with guidance about the rules of the classroom and needs to observe them.

• Both teachers should always treat each other with mutual respect.

Pullout instruction

Pullout instruction—the form of instruction that most people think of when they think about special education—involves pulling students out of the general education classroom to receive at least some of their instruction in a separate space, typically a special education classroom. Pullout instruction is for students who, after attempts to provide instruction for them in the general education classroom have not succeeded, need additional assistance and support to make progress; it is also used for those students whose goals for learning in a particular area differ from those of the rest of the students.

Because this is the form of instruction most people think of for students eligible for special education, it is often assumed that a special education classroom is where all eligible students receive their services. This is not the case. As noted in previous chapters, most students with disabilities are educated most of the time in the general education classroom.

The following suggestions can help you plan and implement services for students who receive pullout instruction:

• *Be mindful of timing.* If possible, work with the special education teacher to determine the best time for students to be pulled out of the general education classroom.

• *Develop an exit signal.* If needed, develop a signal for the students to remind them when they need to leave to go to the special education classroom. A signal gives the students a bit more independence and decreases classroom disruption.

• *Establish a routine.* Having a routine will help the students remember what they are supposed to take when they leave your classroom.

• *Have an exit plan.* Make sure the students have an easy and quiet way to leave the classroom.

• *Keep students informed.* Make note of announcements you made while the students were gone and inform them accordingly when they return.

• *Establish a re-entry routine.* Having students follow a pre-established routine when they come back into the room will minimize distractions.

• *Meet and catch up.* Meet with the students as soon as possible after they come back into the classroom to make sure they know what is occurring and to catch them up with what they missed.

• *Follow up.* Meet with the special education teacher to follow up on any skills that are being developed in the special education classroom that you can reinforce in your classroom.

• *Consult as necessary.* Be available to talk with the special education teacher about any problems or concerns.

• *Report as necessary.* If you notice any problems or concerns, be sure to report them to others on the IEP team.

• *Think ahead.* Realize that some students may be pulled out temporarily and may soon be back in your classroom full-time.

• *Keep gathering data.* Data on any concerns you have or problems the students may be having can inform decisions about possible adjustments to pullout instruction.

Collaboration Within and Outside the School

Working with others from both within and outside the school can be one of the best things you do for students with disabilities. As an IEP team member, it is important that you represent not only the interests of the student with a disability and the other students in your classroom, but also your own interests. The following tips can help you collaborate as effectively as possible:

• *Stay connected with others.* Find out what is going on in other parts of the school and attend meetings; visit the teachers' lounge to keep up with the main topics being discussed. It is difficult to collaborate with others if you do not know what is important to them.

• *Call the parents.* Keep them informed about progress. E-mail is a good way to communicate, but an occasional phone call may elicit important information.

• *Learn names.* Determine who is involved with the student. Learn their names and their preferred methods of engaging.

• *Go to IEP team meetings.* Make a point not only to go to IEP team meetings but also to learn what you can from others beforehand and to know what other team members will be recommending.

• *Seek help.* Remember that you are not alone in providing services for these students; you are a part of a team. When there are problems, let the others know and work with them to create solutions.

• *Be willing to help.* When others need assistance, offer to do what you can for them even if you do not know beforehand how to help.

• *Step out of your comfort zone.* Be willing to work with students whom you may not have worked with before. You also may be asked to implement strategies you have not used in the past and address needs outside of the curriculum.

• *Keep your focus on the student.*

Replacement Curriculum

The curriculum in most schools is based on grade levels or standards. Teachers use materials developed to ensure students are achieving at or near their grade level. This model works well for most students, but some students with disabilities may have problems with a grade-level curriculum and thus may receive instruction based on a replacement curriculum.

A replacement curriculum is completely different from that used in the general education classroom. The topics may be the same or similar, but the level of detail differs. For example, a 7th grade science teacher may pull content from a 4th grade book on the same topic. The reading level will be lower, but the basics of the content will be similar to help the student understand the concepts. The special education teacher typically provides the replacement curriculum, which the general education teacher delivers. This is most often an explicit, structured, systematic, and cumulative program. Because this curriculum corresponds not to traditional grade levels but rather to the student's current ability levels, it can be used with students of any age.

Paraprofessionals

A paraprofessional is someone who helps you with either a specific student or the class as a whole. The paraprofessional reports to you and is responsible for implementing your directions. Here are some suggestions for supervising paraprofessionals and forging a relationship that will best serve students.

• *Create a collaborative, respectful atmosphere.* Treat paraprofessionals as the colleagues they are, and solicit their input working with the students or ways to improve the classroom. You want communication to be open and ideas to be shared. Be mindful that any criticism you provide should be constructive. Set up a safe communication system between yourself and paraprofessionals. They need to be able to safely share their concerns and express their ideas in regard to the students with whom they work.

• *Set expectations.* Make sure you explain to the paraprofessionals what you expect from them as a part of their job. Identify the overall aim or big-picture goal for the student. Clarify what you expect the student to be working on or addressing. Also clarify what you do not want to see from the student (and the paraprofessional). Establish a working environment such that everyone understands their roles in the classroom, and then make clear that you expect them to fulfill those roles.

• *Teach data-gathering techniques.* As we have mentioned several times in this book, data-gathering has an important role in various aspects of educating students with disabilities, and paraprofessionals can help with your data-collection efforts. They might conduct basic observations of frequency of behaviors, duration of behaviors, and even latency of behaviors (see Chapters 2 and 7 for more information on conducting observations). However, it is imperative that you adequately train paraprofessionals on how to gather the data, to ensure consistency and reliability of the information that they collect. If you do not possess this expertise yourself, seek assistance from an administrator.

• *Teach other skills.* Having another person to provide assistance in the classroom will only be beneficial if the person knows the skills the student needs to address, and they understand how to teach the skill. For example, if the paraprofessional will be helping with reading instruction, make sure you teach the paraprofessional the skills you want reinforced with the students. If the concern is behavior management, make sure the paraprofessional understands how to respond to the behavior, what behaviors should be reinforced, which ones can be ignored, and which ones you, the teacher, will have to address. Paraprofessionals need to know not only the skills to be taught but also the manner in which you expect them to teach the skills and how to respond to errors the students may make.

• *Express appreciation.* The paraprofessionals' job is not easy, and the pay is often not very good. Make sure they know how much you appreciate them by saying thank you and ensuring that they feel a valued part of your classroom team.

• *Listen.* Pay attention to the paraprofessionals' concerns and comments about their work with the students.

Given all the responsibilities you have as a general education teacher, having another set of hands to help in the classroom can be a critical factor for ensuring the success of students with disabilities—and other students as well. See Gerlach (2015) for more information on working with paraprofessionals.

Related Services

The purpose of related services is to help students who are eligible for special education access the general education curriculum and become as independent as possible. Although other students might benefit from related services, the only students who are eligible are those receiving special education. Therefore, it is important to remember that students who do not qualify for special education services will not be able to receive a related service. For example, if you have a student who has difficulty with fine motor skills that is adversely affecting her ability to perform in the classroom, this student will only be able to receive services from the occupational therapists if she is qualified under one of the special education categories and has other educational goals in her IEP. This does not mean that you cannot contact the occupational therapist to discuss strategies you might use to help this student, but it will not be an IEP service.

Related services and the IEP

A student may require any of the following related services in order to benefit from special education services. Related services, as listed under IDEA, include (but are not limited to) the following:

- Audiology services
- Counseling services
- Early identification and assessment of disabilities in students
- Medical services
- Occupational therapy
- Orientation and mobility services
- Parent counseling and training
- Physical therapy
- Psychological services
- Recreation
- Rehabilitation counseling services
- School health services
- Social work services in schools
- Speech-language pathology services
- Transportation

After careful review of a student's evaluation, the IEP team determines the specific related service or services the student is to receive (if any) and includes those services in the student's IEP. If a related service is deemed necessary, the appropriate related-service professional should be involved in developing the IEP. That individual may be invited by the school or parent to join the IEP team as a person with "knowledge or special expertise regarding the child" [§300.321(a)(6)].

Goals are written for a related service just as they are for other special education services. The IEP must also specify the following factors with respect to each service:

When the service will begin
How often it will be provided and for what amount of time
Where it will be provided [§300.320(a)(7)]

Keep in mind that a student with a disability may not require a related service, or the student may require a combination of services. All students should be treated individually. The list of related services presented here is not exhaustive, and other developmental, corrective, or supportive services may be required to help a student with a disability benefit from special education.

Once the type and amount of related services are noted in the student's IEP, the school district must ensure that all of the related services specified are, in fact, provided. Changes in the amount or type of services listed in the IEP cannot be made without another IEP meeting.

Working with related-service personnel

In addition to providing specific kinds of support for teachers and help for students, related-service personnel do the following:

- Provide prevention and intervention services in schools
- Work with administrators
- Work to improve classroom-management skills
- Work to remove barriers to learning
- Consult with parents
- Provide various instructional strategies
- Provide a continuum of support. (ASHA, 2015)

Although, as noted, many different types of professionals work as related-service providers, certain general principles apply in relation to your interactions with them. Here are some general tips for working with related-service providers:

- *Be welcoming.* Many related-service providers travel from school to school. Do what you can to make them feel welcome at your school and invite them to school activities. They are a part of the school. Make them feel that way.
- *Treat them as professionals.* Related-service providers have specific knowledge and skills in their area that can help the student make progress in the curriculum. They are a wonderful resource, and some of their suggestions for students with disabilities may actually help you with many other students in your classroom.
- *Suggest an observation.* Invite the related-service providers to observe the student in the classroom and see how the student is functioning compared to peers.

• *Collaborate.* The related-service providers are working primarily with the student but will need to work with you to determine additional problems and successes. Talk with the related-service providers about your classroom schedule, the student's preferred activities, and aspects of the curriculum that are causing problems for the student. Share with them issues and concerns you may notice. Remember, you likely will be working with the student more hours per week than a related-service provider will. Talk with the provider about skills or strategies you should implement or any other follow-through activities you can provide for the student.

• *Be responsive.* Respond promptly to related-services providers' questions and concerns and any requests for more information about how the student is doing.

• *Schedule follow-up meetings.* Whenever a related-services provider meets with the student, arrange a short meeting to make sure you are up to date about any issues or problems. Write down concerns to share at this meeting.

• *Respect their time.* Many related-services providers have heavy schedules and must work with multiple students within a short time frame. Respect this reality, and arrange meetings to talk with them about issues at times that are convenient for them.

Providers of Outside Services

Some districts contract with outside individuals or agencies to provide services for students with disabilities. They may do so because there are very few students who need these services, there are too few service providers within the district, or contracting is more cost effective. Contracted services can include occupational therapy, tutoring, transportation, and many of the related services mentioned earlier. All of the suggested tips listed for working with related-services providers are applicable to working with providers of outside services as well.

Summary

Students with disabilities receive varying types and amounts of services, and this range of placement, called the "continuum of services," may change as the students' needs change. The goal is always to provide services in the least restrictive environment, as required by law. Services may be provided in the general education classroom through consultation, collaboration, or coteaching by teachers; or through push-in instruction, in which the special education teacher or other staff works in the regular classroom. Pullout instruction, in which the student is removed from the regular classroom, is appropriate only if all other alternatives have failed to provide the desired results or if the student has truly unique needs.

Collaborating with others—related-service personnel, outside service providers, and paraprofessionals—is an important aspect of educating students with disabilities. In all cases, treating these individuals with respect and establishing effective channels of two-way communication are important considerations.

9

Assessment, Grades, Graduation, and Diplomas

Assessing students is an important component of education today. Tests are used to determine student progress, eligibility for services, and, increasingly, teacher and school effectiveness. The assessment of students with disabilities brings unique challenges in terms of grading, report cards, graduation, and standardized assessments. Understanding the differences and addressing the needs of students with disabilities will help you maximize student performance and use tests and assessments to evaluate performance more accurately.

This chapter focuses on district, state, and classroom-based assessments given to all students, and how these relate to students with disabilities. For information on the assessment process for determining eligibility for special education, see Chapter 2.

Assessment

Although there are many ways to classify the kinds of assessment used in education, we'd like to begin with the simple distinction of formal versus informal. *Formal assessments* are systematic methods to ascertain what students have learned. They are often tied to standards and can be used to compare a student's functioning to that of other students. Mandated statewide assessments are perhaps the most obvious example. Formal assessments often have standardized administration procedures and standardized scoring. *Informal assessments* are those used by teachers to determine a student's level of functioning in a classroom. They include no standardized procedures for administration and scoring. Teachers use informal assessments to check in with students throughout the day, as when they ask students about math facts or their knowledge of vowel sounds, or inquire about whether a student has written down the homework assignment.

The Every Student Succeeds Act of 2015 mandates formal assessment of all students. The purpose of the assessment is to hold districts accountable for the education of students and to ensure they are advancing toward grade-level achievement. High-stakes standardized tests can best be defined as tests that include scoring used to make major decisions about students, including retention in grade and graduation.

Students eligible for special education may get accommodations on the various assessments, or they can be given alternative assessments, if necessary, but states differ in how they handle this situation.

Accommodations

The goal of accommodations is to ensure that the assessment is, to the extent possible, accessing the student's knowledge; the goal is *not* to demonstrate how the disability is affecting the student's learning (Bolt, 2004a). This concept is important for the IEP team—and especially the general education teacher— to consider. The accommodations needed to ensure that the disability is not negatively affecting the assessment results are determined by the IEP team and included in the IEP or Section 504 document. As the general education teacher, you have a significant role in determining the appropriate accommodations. The most frequently allowed testing accommodations include the use of dictated response, large print, Braille, extended time, and sign-language interpretation for instructions (Bolt, 2004b).

The best advice we can offer about accommodations is to think about them long before the assessments are actually administered. The IEP or Section 504 plan should include a list of the accommodations

IMPORTANT POINTS

- Assessments are a key component of any education program.

- Students with disabilities need accommodations for some tests.

- It is important to consider what assessments are given to students with disabilities and the desired outcomes.

- Students with disabilities are to receive updates on the goals and objectives of their IEPs with the same frequency that typically developing peers receive report cards.

- Some students with disabilities will require modified grading.

- Some students with disabilities may have modified graduation requirements.

that will be used, and they must be consistent with the process for instruction and assessment used in the classroom for the student with a disability. Further, the accommodations are based on student need, not disability type. Just because a student has a certain disability does not mean the student requires the same accommodations as another student with the same disability (Bolt, 2004b). Finally, the examiner must note all accommodations used to ensure alignment with the student's IEP.

Accommodations can be broken down into various categories: location, time, materials, and procedures. Although the information in Figure 9.1 is not comprehensive, it can help an IEP team make an informed decision about possible accommodations for the student.

Figure 9.1 / Examples of Assessment Accommodations

Location Accommodations

- In a separate room, individually
- In a separate room, with a small group
- In a special education classroom
- At home or the homebound location
- In a separate setting, such as a hospital
- In a space with special noise-reduction features
- In a space with special lighting
- In a space with special desks (e.g., a standing desk or a study carrel)
- Seated near the examiner

Time Accommodations

- Additional time, as needed
- Frequent breaks
- Early termination (only when the student cannot complete any additional sections)

Materials Accommodations

- Large print
- Braille
- Audio recording
- High-contrast paper

Procedural Accommodations

- Test questions read aloud
- Test directions read aloud
- Directions using sign language
- Directions using cued speech
- Amplification devices
- Covering part of the test to reduce stimuli
- Rewording of directions
- Calculator for math sections
- Manipulatives for math sections
- Use of graph paper allowed
- Familiar examiner
- Dictation of responses
- Marking answers in test book for others to transfer

In addition to the accommodations, it is important to ensure that students with disabilities are well-prepared to take the assessment. Make sure students have eaten and have taken any prescribed medications. Make sure those who wear eyeglasses or hearing aids have those devices. Students who need amplification should receive appropriate practice with the devices, and those who use interpreters for sign language should be facing the interpreter. Taking steps such as these can help students with disabilities perform to the best of their ability on assessments.

Alternative assessment

Although IDEA and ESSA mandate that all students receiving services must be assessed as a part of the state assessment process, those who have more severe disabilities can be administered an alternative exam. Typically the determining factor for an alternative assessment is the nature of the student's disability, specifically whether it is so severe that the student is not receiving instruction in the knowledge and skills the general statement assessment measures (for example, if the student could not complete the types of questions included on the test, even with accommodations and modifications). Depending on individual state requirements, the alternative assessment may not have to be administered in every content area.

Grades and Report Cards

Report cards are an integral part of the educational system, and all students, including those with disabilities, are expected to receive a report card providing information about progress. Follow your district's policy on determining and reporting grades and adhere to the local standards. Many district policies for students with disabilities reflect grading procedures delineated in the IEP and include making notations on the report card itself to indicate that the grade reflects the student's performance with accommodations.

There are no federal guidelines or procedures in the area of grades and report cards for students with disabilities, so each determination will need to be made individually. The following points are intended to help guide you as you make the determination for the specific students in your classes.

Student need. Not all students with disabilities need modified grades or an alternate curriculum. Determine if the student is functioning close to or on grade level and if accommodations in grading might be necessary. Some students would not receive passing grades on assignments or classes without accommodations or modifications. Accommodations are intended to level the playing field so that the grade can truly reflect what the student knows and the student's progress in the curriculum. The IEP team, with the general education teacher playing a major role, makes the determination of need.

District policy. Does the district have a policy on the reporting of grades for students receiving special education? If so, does it delineate responsibilities and notations, or does it specifically state how grades are to be reported? If the policy does not specifically address students with special needs, then the policies that are in place for all students must be followed.

IEP. If the IEP team determines the student will require modified grading, modified grading needs to be followed by all teachers unless the IEP team determines otherwise. Is the student to be graded based on progress toward goals and objectives? Is the student to be graded on progress in the general education curriculum? These questions should be covered in the IEP.

Grade for attempts. Instead of reporting solely the final grade the student receives on the assignment or class, at times it may be appropriate to give greater weight to attempts and effort than the final product. You may choose to give extra points if students worked really hard and continued to try even though they might not have been able to demonstrate mastery of the goals or objectives. If students can demonstrate successful performance, this is an *inappropriate* accommodation. But for some students and their parents, participation is very important, and you should strive to help the students be a part of the class as much as possible.

Performance contracts. Some students with disabilities, despite your efforts, will be unable to demonstrate mastery of content in a general education classroom to the same degree as most other students. An alternative is to develop a contract for such students on specific activities that they will have to perform related to the activities of the classroom. If they complete these specified activities, they will receive a certain grade.

Individual grading plans. Based on the activities and goals of a student's IEP, you can assign grades for performance of specific accomplishments or on percentage of progress toward the goals. This can be done with students with more severe intellectual disabilities who might be unlikely or unable to demonstrate mastery in a manner consistent with the grading system in a general education classroom. As with all grading modifications, the student's IEP team should discuss this matter.

Graduation for Students with IEPs

Increasingly, policy makers are calling for every student who graduates from high school to be college or career ready (U.S. Department of Education,

2012). Many students eligible for special education and related services can meet traditional graduation requirements with few or no accommodations and graduate with their chronologically aged peers. However, some students with disabilities will have an extremely difficult time meeting, or may be unable to meet, the traditional graduation requirements.

States vary in their specific requirements for graduation, so you will need to consult your individual state for information. However, it is important to remember that students with disabilities have the right to receive a diploma to the same extent as students without disabilities. Some states or districts offer only a standard diploma, whereas others may offer a range of diplomas. The most common types of diplomas include the honors diploma, standard or regular diploma, certificate of completion/attendance, certificate of achievement, and occupational diploma (Johnson, Thurlow, & Stout, 2007).

Keep in mind that according to federal regulations, students with disabilities continue to be eligible for FAPE until they have met the requirements for a "regular diploma or until they have reached the age at which eligibility ceases under the age requirements of the state" (Individuals with Disabilities Education Act, 2004). The IEP team should ensure that the IEP is aligned with the interests and goals the student has for postsecondary life, be it college, a career, or independent living. All efforts to get a regular diploma should be exhausted before an alternate diploma is considered. Requirements for regular diplomas will also depend on the state and district policies.

The following questions (guided by the work of Johnson, Thurlow, Cosia, & Bremer, 2005) can be used as a guide when considering alternative routes to graduation for students eligible for special education. Not all of the questions will apply, but considering them will help you and your colleagues on the IEP team make an informed decision about the graduation options.

- What is the student's disability?
- How does the student's disability limit, or potentially limit, the completion of graduation requirements without accommodations?
- What accommodations are allowed in the classroom while earning a standard diploma?
- Is an exit test required?
- What accommodations are allowed while taking the exit test?
- Will the student receive instruction aligned with the test questions?
- Are alternative diplomas available? If so, what are the requirements, characteristics, advantages, and disadvantages of each?

• Are portfolios or other projects accepted as indicators of student learning and skills as an optional pathway to a diploma?

• Is successful completion of federally mandated standardized assessments required for graduation?

• What are the alternatives to the successful completion of standardized assessments?

The last two questions listed bring up an important point. As we noted earlier in this chapter, in most states, students eligible for special education and related services must take the state standardized assessments mandated by federal legislation. Although a student's IEP team cannot exempt a student with a disability from participating in a statewide assessment, the team must determine whether special accommodations in the administration of the test are necessary to permit the student to participate. Some states require a proficient score in order to graduate with a standard diploma. However, depending on the state, regardless of whether they are proficient on the standardized examination, students eligible for special education can still be eligible for a standard diploma if the IEP team concludes they have satisfactorily completed their special education programs.

Given the variations among states and districts regarding graduation requirements and diploma options, teachers of students with disabilities, IEP team members, and parents should become aware of the specific requirements of their state or district, use the questions provided here, and make decisions based on the student's goals, including their post-school goals. (See Chapter 6 for more information on helping students get ready for postschool life.)

Leaving School

Students eligible for special education services can stay in school until age 21 (19 in Maine and Montana). Typically, a student who accepts a diploma before age 21 may no longer stay in school. When a student is about to leave school, the parents need to be notified, because this is considered a change in placement under the law. In most states, districts are not obligated to do a reevaluation before the student exits school, but the district is required to provide a summary of the student's academic achievement and functional performance, and should also include recommendations on how the student could achieve the postsecondary goals outlined in the IEP.

Some students will choose to leave school when their chronologically aged peers leave school, and unless the parent (depending on the state) has retained guardianship rights, the students can make their own educational decisions. This affords the students the rights that the parents previously had.

Students may leave school for a variety of reasons, including health or family needs or simply not wanting to stay in school long enough to receive a diploma. For these students, an alternative for high school equivalency is the GED, or General Educational Development. The GED consists of a series of tests used to determine whether the student has a high school graduate's level of knowledge. Some states use the TASC (Test Assessing Secondary Completion) or the HiSET (High School Equivalency Test). Again, you need to determine which tests are administered in your state.

Students with disabilities can receive accommodations on the GED assessment as long as they meet one or more of the following criteria (the TASC and HiSET have similar criteria and accommodations):

- Are age 17
- Have a physical disability
- Have visual impairment
- Have a hearing impairment
- Have a learning disability
- Have a cognitive disability
- Have ADHD

More information is available at the GED website: www.gedtestingservice.com/testers-accommodations-for-disability.

Summary

Testing and grading students with disabilities is controversial. The purpose of testing and providing grades is to help students and parents to understand the student's progress in the curriculum. Many students with disabilities need no additional assistance to access the curriculum and can be provided grades in the same manner as typically developing students. Others, however, require additional supports for accessing the information they are to be tested on, as well as modifications in grading. Graduation for some students with disabilities can be challenging, based on the state and district requirements prescribed for all students. It is important to consider accommodations not only for graduation but also for mandatory state assessments and for the GED/TASC/HiSET. The decision about what type of accommodation a student needs is an IEP team responsibility and needs to be made based on the individual needs of the student and not on the disability.

10
Putting It All Together

Throughout this book we have highlighted the importance of the general education teacher's role in providing services for students with disabilities. Often they are the first ones to notice that a student needs assistance. The data they collect are used to make the initial referral for testing for special education and to help determine the level of functioning of the student compared to peers, which makes the case for determining eligibility for special education and related services. After the evaluation is completed and the student is found eligible, general education teachers often provide the majority of educational services the student receives. Their importance in working with students who receive special education cannot be overstated. In this chapter we summarize and reiterate key points related to what you, as a general education teacher, need to know to work effectively with students with disabilities.

Roles and Responsibilities

Given that general education teachers have a key role in providing services to students with disabilities, it is helpful to clarify their various roles and responsibilities and to highlight certain points. In this section, we briefly describe key aspects of the work (each of which we have also discussed in other parts of this book).

Planning curriculum. As the general education teacher, you are the curriculum specialist on the IEP team. You know the current curriculum and understand how to plan for and implement it. For students with disabilities, this may require accommodations and modifications, but in any case, effective planning before instruction is important, as are reflecting on student progress, noting effective strategies for the individual student, and making programming recommendations to allow the student to be successful in the least restrictive environment possible.

Working with families. Often the only school-related names parents know are those of their child's general education teacher and the school principal. They may know the names of the special education teacher and related-service personnel, but they often view the general education teacher as their child's main teacher (which is often the case). They will look to you for information and guidance. Therefore it is imperative that you be present, ask questions at IEP and Section 504 meetings, be able to answer queries from parents at a later date, and be able to explain to them the specifics of the plan developed for their child. If you do not know the specifics, do what it takes to get the answers for the parents.

Administering standardized assessments. Increasingly, teachers are being evaluated based on their students' scores on standardized assessments. As noted in Chapter 9, some students with disabilities can get accommodations for these assessments, and part of your job is to make recommendations to the IEP team regarding these accommodations. Another important part of your role is the preparation and training you give the students to help them maximize their potential and to reduce their anxiety over the tests.

Contributing to annual reports. IEPs and Section 504 plans are to be reviewed annually. You should come to the review meeting prepared to discuss how the student performed in your class. Bring data on student performance, how the student compared to others in the class, and successful instructional strategies, as well as recommendations for accommodations and modifications. Also come prepared to discuss recommendations for improvement in

IMPORTANT POINTS

- The general education teacher is a major player on the special education team for a student with a disability.

- The general education teacher's role is often to serve as a central access point for all the other professionals who work with the student.

- The general education teacher should seek assistance when necessary to address student needs.

- The general education teacher is expected to be an active participant in all IEP or Section 504 team meetings.

- The general education teacher should be provided the necessary information from a student's IEP or Section 504 plan to ensure appropriate delivery of services.

services for the next year based on your observations and data. You may be advocating for more or fewer services, based on the student's current level of functioning and the classroom and curricular requirements. Also be ready to discuss how the student is viewed socially in the classroom.

Serving as point person. Some students receiving special education and related services have multiple individuals working with them. These individuals, because of their schedules, may see each other only at meetings. It is important as a point person to help relay information and to discuss problems with the various professionals who are in and out of the classroom. They will likely ask for updates about performance and seek clarification of problems since their last visit. Be ready with notices and updates for them.

Providing continuity. As the point person, you may be the one continuous presence for many students with disabilities. Providing this continuity is important for many students' educational needs, but it is also important for the other professionals to understand. The need for continuity is why you must prepare any substitute who will come into your classroom with information about the various needs of the students with disabilities, and the potential comings and goings of the professionals throughout the day. The substitute will also need to know about academic accommodations and any medical needs of the students.

Respecting confidentiality. You will learn a lot of detailed information about the students, their lives, and their families. It is very important to share the information only with those who need to know it in order to work with the student. For example, if a student has allergic reactions, it is important to alert substitute teachers to this situation and make them aware of what to look for and their expected response.

Seeking professional development. Some students will have disabilities that are very rare. You may never see this disability and its specific needs again in your teaching career, but you will need to learn about it to help the student progress in the curriculum and succeed at school. Changes will also occur in special education laws and regulations, including differing requirements for the assessment of all students. It is imperative to keep abreast of changes and updates. Organizations to join include ASCD (www.ascd.org), the Council for Exceptional Children (www.cec.sped.org), and others dedicated to supporting professionals working with students with disabilities. The Internet is a repository for a lot of information, but much of it is not vetted, and you may find yourself uncertain about the veracity and professionalism of the content. Joining an organization such as ASCD or CEC will help you keep up to date and knowledgeable about how to provide effective instruction for all students, not just those with disabilities.

In addition, you may need to provide professional development for others about the nature and needs of a student in your classroom and the student's specific disability. The education of students with disabilities is a whole-school responsibility. The PE teacher will need to know what to watch for and how to deal with possible emergencies, as will the librarian, the classroom paraprofessional/aide, the art teacher, the bus driver, and possible substitute teachers. If the student has a medical condition that is rare and requires special assistance, work with your school nurse and special education staff to provide appropriate and necessary information to those who have responsibility for the student.

Keeping records. One of the complaints about special education is how paperwork intensive it is (Bateman, 2005). However, there are very clear reasons to document and furnish details about services provided and progress made (or not made), to ensure that a student with a disability receives an appropriate education. You will be expected to maintain accurate and complete student records and to prepare reports on children and activities as required by laws, district policies, and administrative regulations. Keeping records helps with planning and programming.

Handling emergencies. Not everything will go as planned. There may be times when a student has a medical need that you will have to help address. There may be times when the team has worked to include a student in a class and it is clear the plan is not working, and there may be times when unexpected behaviors arise that require an immediate intervention. Issues will need to be addressed, even if they fall outside the student's plan. Remember that any member of an IEP team can call for a meeting.

Advocating for the student. Every member of the IEP team is an advocate for the student; however, as the classroom teacher, you are the school staff member who best knows the student and how the disability affects the student's learning. The student may be eligible for special education services, but you will need to tell others on the IEP team the *specific* needs the student has in relation to others in your classroom and the problems encountered. Represent the student at meetings, be willing to ask questions about the specifics of the program, and then be able to explain this information to others, including parents. Many parents do not know what goes on in a school day-to-day, and therefore they may be unable to formulate questions about the specifics of a student's program.

Filling a critical role on the IEP team. Based on the information provided in this book, the importance of being an effective and participatory team member should be obvious.

Serving as behavior interventionist. Because you likely are with the student more than other professionals, you will have to teach appropriate behavior skills. By employing techniques in an overall positive behavioral support system, you will have to teach socially acceptable behavior as determined by the student's IEP. You will have to do this when other students are present and while observing the student with a disability interacting with peers.

Taking initiative and dealing with the unexpected. Inevitably you will encounter issues, problems, and needs that you—and others—did not anticipate. An important part of your role is to step up to the challenge and do what you can to improve the situation. Remember that your overarching goal is to meet students' needs so they can focus on learning and make progress in the curriculum.

Teaching

Much of what we recognize as "good teaching" benefits all students. However, it is helpful to understand certain unique situations and requirements when teaching students with disabilities.

Implementing special education strategies. As discussed in other chapters of this book, students with disabilities will have either an IEP or a 504 plan. These documents will delineate specific instructional methods and strategies that you will need to implement. There may also be specific strategies the special education teacher, the speech language pathologist, or the occupational therapist will ask you to reinforce to help the student continue to make progress between visits with those professionals. You are expected to carry out these requirements at the same time you are working with perhaps 25 or more other students in the classroom. Although the prospect may seem overwhelming, remember that many of the strategies you learn by working with students with disabilities will also enhance your overall teaching skills and the learning of all students in your classroom. Take this opportunity to improve your craft and become a stronger educator.

Using a variety of techniques. We know that students do not all learn in the same way, and you are expected to try different methods or techniques when working with all students, including those with disabilities. You may need to provide more explanation, more examples, or more repetition for students with disabilities than you do for other students. The goal is always to help all students understand the concepts and learn from the material you present.

Modifying the curriculum. You may have to modify the curriculum by changing the amount of information presented or the number of questions you expect students with disabilities to answer, or you may have to use different instructional materials to help them access the curriculum. At the same time, it is best not to assume that accommodations or modifications will be necessary for every subject and every lesson. Your careful evaluation of students should make clear which areas require such changes.

Balancing students' time. You will need to plan and conduct activities that ensure a balanced program of instruction, demonstration, and work time. All students, including those with disabilities, need opportunities to observe, question, and investigate.

Providing clarity. It is your responsibility to develop clear objectives for the lessons, and clear examples and nonexamples of the expected work products, classroom processes, and behavioral expectations. Communicating this information to students enables them to know exactly what is expected of them and how they will be required to perform. Give students a sense of how long the lesson and related activities will last. Help them with planning and understanding the time frame and material to be covered.

Communicating. Keep others—especially parents, special education teachers, and the principal—informed about classroom-related problems and concerns. You do not want to go to an IEP review at the end of the year and tell the parents for the first time that the student has not made any progress in your class, or make proposals regarding concerns that other team members are not aware of. You also want to make sure the principal knows of any problems so that if the parents call the principal, he or she has some knowledge of the issues and can make informed statements regarding the student's education.

Collaborating. Close collaboration is essential for meeting student needs. You will rely on others for advice about best practices and strategies, and you should expect to foster a strong working relationship with school staff, parents, and providers of outside services.

Talk with others about successes as well as difficulties. Too often we focus on problems and forget to celebrate successes. In addition, programs can be developed or modified based on successful strategies.

Finally, if there is a problem that needs to be addressed and the student is clearly not making progress or has behavior problems that are preventing learning, make sure the members of the IEP team are aware and a meeting is called to discuss any needed changes. The IEP team can act only if you inform them about any problems and concerns you have.

Expectations

As we've noted many times, students with disabilities have a team of individuals working on their behalf, so you are never alone in this endeavor. In the Introduction to this book we discussed some of the expectations you should have in working with others. Here we provide greater detail about what to expect from supervisors and administrators, as well as what students expect from their teachers.

What teachers can expect from supervisors and administrators

Administrators and supervisors have a responsibility to support classroom teachers. Do not shy away from asking for help. Your questions also help them to understand the challenges classroom teachers are experiencing.

Support. When you have questions or concerns about a student in your classroom, an administrator—be it the principal, the curriculum director, or the special education supervisor—should be able to help. If administrators or supervisors do not have immediate answers, they should work with you to find solutions. They should also support you when there are issues related to discipline, grades, or other matters that come up when talking with parents. If there are differences in opinion or concerns about how a situation was handled, these should be discussed with the administrators before any parent or staff meetings.

Resources. Funding is a challenge for districts of all types and sizes. Talk with your administrator about what you need in order to provide for the needs of a student. The administrator should work with you to acquire those resources or to develop other plans to meet the student's needs.

Encouragement. In every job, some days are clearly better than others, and on the tough days, supervisors should provide encouragement and moral support for the work you are doing. They can also provide advice about how to address tough situations and help you plan for future issues that may come up.

Reasonable expectations. Supervisors and administrators should have high standards for performance, so that schools can become the best they can be. These individuals should provide clarity about the district's expectations for classroom management and student learning, forms and frequency of communication, and specific school policies. They should also help teachers—particularly new teachers—understand the unwritten rules that go along with working in a specific district. Are there certain parking places informally reserved for school board members in the parking lot? How frequently are teachers expected to bring food to the teachers' lounge to share with others? What are reasonable expectations for attendance during in-service days? What is the accepted procedure if a teacher has to leave class to go to the bathroom? Typically this information is not written down, but it can help a new teacher get through a year without causing problems for others.

Understanding. Supervisors and administrators should understand what is going on in the classroom in terms of the sizable number of interactions and the weighty responsibilities teachers take on when working with students. Quality teachers are paying attention to many different things at once, and multitasking is one of a teacher's most important skills. Understanding this reality and providing support for all that teachers are required to do is important because it means that administrators and supervisors acknowledge that teaching is a hard job—but also that when it is done right, it can help change students' lives.

What students can expect of their teachers

Much has been written about what students expect from teachers, but it can be distilled down to three things: to be knowledgeable, to be able to clearly explain that knowledge, and to care about students as people. Other desirable attributes that people often suggest include wanting a teacher to provide inspiration and to take all questions seriously, but here we focus on the first three, because the others can be subsumed under those.

Knowledge. Think back to the teachers you have liked. They probably had considerable knowledge about what they were teaching, as well as a passion or desire to help others understand the content. This does not mean that you have to be passionate about everything you teach, but you do need to help students understand how concepts relate to each other, and therefore your own understanding of the material is both necessary and powerful.

The ability to explain. You may have had teachers who were extremely knowledgeable about the content but either could not explain the concepts to others or did not connect with their audience. As a general education teacher, it is important that you understand the individual concepts (and how they relate to other concepts you will be teaching in the future) and embed them in lessons that are engaging to students and that include just enough detail to ensure that students understand and can apply what they have learned. This is a critical skill that you should seek to develop throughout your teaching career.

Care. You are one of the most important people in your students' lives, so it is important to not only care about the students but to let them know you care. Become interested in their activities, ask them about their fashion preferences and things going on at home and with friends, and talk to them about their extracurricular activities. But also watch for signs of problems, such as not eating, bruises, or dramatic changes in behavior. As we have stated many times in this book, you will be the teacher who knows and interacts with the students more than any other adult, their parents excepted. As a result, you will have many opportunities to notice concerns, communicate with others, and work as an IEP team member to address the needs of the students. Doing so is an important expression of the care you have for them.

Parting Thoughts

We began this book by noting that working with students with disabilities can be challenging, but also very rewarding. Students with disabilities, whether they have an IEP or a Section 504 plan, deserve an education, and the information in this book will help you to make that possible. We encourage you to embrace the opportunities for growth that working with students with disabilities will provide you, both as a person and as a professional.

Appendix A
Special Education Terms and Acronyms

ABA—Applied behavior analysis

ABC analysis—Analysis of antecedents, behaviors, and consequences

ability grouping—Clustering students based on past performance

academic aptitude—The ability to do schoolwork; sometimes called "scholastic aptitude"

accommodations—Changes in how material is taught or a test is administered

accountability—Holding schools responsible for student performance

achievement/ability discrepancy—The difference between where the student is functioning and where we expect the student to be functioning; used to help identify learning disabilities

achievement gap—The difference in performance between different groups

achievement test—A test measuring competency in a particular skill or academic area

acuity—How well a person sees or hears

ADA—Americans with Disabilities Act of 1990.

adaptive behavior—Behavior related to how well a person interacts with his or her environment

ADD—Attention deficit disorder

ADHD—Attention deficit hyperactivity disorder

ADL—Activities of daily living

administrative due process hearing—A hearing to resolve disputes between parents and school districts

AE—Age equivalent

alternate achievement standards—Standards that are different for students of the same grade or age

alternative assessments—Nonstandardized assessments, including projects, reports, performances

annual goals—IEP goals that could reasonably be accomplished in a one-year period

APE—Adaptive physical education

articulation—The clarity of a student's speech; speaking

ASD—Autism spectrum disorder

ASL—American Sign Language

assistive technology device—Equipment or technology to help a student with a disability

AT—Assistive technology

audiology—The professional field dedicated to identifying and determining the extent of hearing loss; also, a related service offered to students with hearing loss

auditory discrimination—The ability to distinguish differences in sound

autism spectrum disorder—A condition that includes difficulty with verbal and nonverbal communication and dealing with social interactions

baseline measurement—The starting point of reference for measuring something; used, for example, in recording the frequency of a behavior

BD—Behavior, or behavioral, disorder

behavior disorder (BD)—Synonym for emotional disturbance

behavior intervention plan (BIP)—A plan of positive behavioral supports

behavioral objective—A description of what a student will do, in measurable terms

BIP—Behavior intervention plan

CA—Chronological age

CAPD—Central auditory processing disorder

categorical placement—Identifying a student for special education services based on his or her IDEA eligibility category

CBA—Curriculum-based assessment

CBM—Curriculum-based measurement

CD—Cognitive disability

CD—Communication disorder

CF—Cystic fibrosis

child find—How schools seek out and identify all students with disabilities in their area

community-based—Refers to skills taught in locations in the community

compensatory education—Services provided to make up for what the child has missed

consent—The requirement and expectation that parents be fully informed about their child's educational program

COTA—Certified occupational therapy assistant

CP—Cerebral palsy

criterion-referenced tests (CRTs)—Tests that compare how a child does compared to an established criterion

CRT—Criterion-referenced test

cumulative file—The file containing all the documents a school has on a child

curriculum-based assessment—An assessment that measures a child's progress in the curriculum

DD—Developmental delay

deaf-blindness—Significant hearing and vision loss

deafness—A significant hearing impairment

delay—Development not within typical time frames

developmental delay—A delay in either intellectual or physical development

diagnostic test—A test to determine a student's strengths or weaknesses

DIBELS—Dynamic Indicators of Basic Early Literacy Skills

disability—A physical or mental condition limiting a person's movements, senses, or activities

DSM-5—*Diagnostic and Statistical Manual of Mental Disorders*, 5th Edition

due process—A process that includes an impartial hearing to determine if a student with a disability is receiving a free appropriate public education

early and periodic screening, diagnosis, and treatment (EPSDT)—Preventive health care for Medicaid-eligible students

early intervening services—Non–special education services to help students who have academic needs

early intervention (EI)—Services for preschool-age children who have academic or developmental needs

ED—Emotional disturbance

EI—Early intervention

ELL—English language learner; also called EL, for English learner

emotional disturbance (ED)—One of the categories of special education

EPSDT—Early and periodic screening, diagnosis, and treatment

ESSA—Every Student Succeeds Act of 2015

ESY—Extended school year services; typically provided during summer

executive functioning—The ability to regulate cognitive processes

extended school day—A time frame longer than a traditional school day, for providing services

facilitated IEP meeting—An IEP meeting led by an impartial person

FAPE—Free appropriate public education; special education services, free to families

FAS—Fetal alcohol syndrome

FBA—Functional behavioral assessment

FERPA—Family Educational Rights and Privacy Act of 1974; a federal law regulating confidentiality of information

fine motor—Referring to movement of small muscles of the body, such as those in the fingers

frustration level—The level at which a student starts to make errors

functional curriculum—A curriculum focusing on life skills

functional goal—A goal to help with a student's performance in the curriculum

GE—Grade equivalent

GLE—Grade-level expectations

gross motor—Referring to movement of the major muscles of the body, such as those in the arms and legs

heterogeneous grouping—Grouping together students with diverse abilities

HI—Hearing impairment

high-stakes tests—Tests that determine tracking or graduation

higher-order thinking skills—Thinking that involves significant cognitive processing, such as critical, reflective, and creative thinking

HIV—Human immunodeficiency virus

home instruction—Home-based services for a student with an IEP

homogeneous grouping—Grouping together students with similar abilities

IAES—Interim alternative educational setting; used for short-term, discipline-related removals

ID—Intellectual disability

IDEA—Individuals with Disabilities Education Act; federal law regarding education for students with disability, most recently reauthorized in 2004

IEE—Independent educational evaluation

IEP—Individualized education program

IEP team—The team that develops and oversees a student's IEP

IFSP—Individualized Family Service Plan; educational plan for students with disabilities who are 3 or younger

independent level—The level at which a student has demonstrated mastery

instructional level—The level at which a student still requires assistance

intellectual disability—One of the IDEA categories of special education; formerly "mental retardation"

interest inventory—A test to identify interests and help a student determine transition activities

interpreter services—Services for students or parents who are deaf or hard of hearing to assist them in understanding content

IQ—Intelligence quotient

ITP—Individualized transition plan

IWRP—Individualized written rehabilitation plan

LD—Learning disability

LEA—Local education agency (your local school district)

learning disability (LD)—One of the IDEA categories of special education

least restrictive environment (LRE)—The requirement of federal law that students with disabilities be placed, to the maximum extent possible, with same-age peers

LEP—Limited English proficient, or limited English proficiency

LRE—Least restrictive environment

LTO—Long-term objective

MA—Mental age

manifestation determination—A process to determine if a student's behavior is caused by the student's disability; completed as part of an IEP team meeting

MDE—Multidisciplinary evaluation

MDT—Multidisciplinary team

mediation—A process for voluntarily settling disputes with the assistance of an impartial outside person

modifications—Changes to what a student is expected to demonstrate

multiple disabilities—Referring to a student with more than one disability

NOS—Not otherwise specified

NVLD—Nonverbal learning disabilities

objective test—Multiple-choice or true/false test

occupational therapy—A related service focusing on a student's fine-motor skills with the intention of moving the student toward independence

OCD—Obsessive compulsive disorder

ODD—Oppositional defiant disorder

OHI—Other health impaired

OI—Orthopedic impairment

orientation and mobility services—Services for individuals who are blind to help with safe movement in schools

orthopedic impairment—A physical disability

OT—Occupational therapy

other health impaired—Having limited strength, vitality, or alertness, including a heightened alertness to environmental stimuli that results in limited alertness with respect to the educational environment

PBIS—Positive behavioral interventions and supports

PBSP—Positive behavioral support plan

PCA—Personal care attendant

PDD—Pervasive developmental disorder

PDD-NOS—Pervasive developmental disorder, not otherwise specified

PLAAFP—Present level of academic achievement and functional performance

PLEP—Present level of educational performance

PLOP—Present level of performance

present level of academic achievement and functional performance—A statement in the IEP describing a student's current level of functioning

prior written notice—Referring to the requirement to provide parents with written information about program changes before those changes begin

procedural safeguards notice—Notice that informs parents of their rights as related to special education procedures

psychological services—Related services that can help assess and work with students on behavioral and emotional issues

psychological test—Test, such as an IQ test, used to determine a child's functioning level

PT—Physical therapy

pullout programs—Programs that remove a child from the classroom for part of a day for special education services

PWN—Prior written notice

qualified examiner—A person licensed to perform evaluation

RAD— Reactive attachment disorder

raw score—The number of test items answered correctly

readiness test—A test to determine if a student is ready for either a certain grade or certain skills

receptive language—The ability to attach meaning to words and phrases

recoupment—The amount of time a student takes to regain skills after an extended break

referral—The notice to a school and parent that a student might need special education

regression—The amount of skill (or skills) a student loses over an extended break

rehabilitation counseling services—Services that focus on career development; may include vocational rehabilitation services

related services—Supportive services as required to help a child with a disability to benefit from special education

resource room—A room dedicated to special education services, where a student with disabilities may spend part of the school day

RTI—Response to intervention

school health services—A related service supplying health services that are designed to enable a child with a disability to receive FAPE as described in the child's IEP

screening—Brief, preliminary testing to determine a child's level of functioning; may be used to determine if additional assessments are necessary

SDI—Specially designed instruction

SEA—State education agency

self-contained placement—Placement in which a student receives educational services most (or all) of the time in a separate classroom

serious emotional disturbance—One of the IDEA categories of special education

services plan—Written document describing services a student is to receive

short-term objectives—Small-scale components that are part of an annual or long-term objective

SLP—Speech language pathologist

specific learning disability—One of the categories of special education

speech-language pathology services—A related service to help students with speech language impairments

SS—Scaled score or standard score

standard score—A score reflecting the number of standard deviations away from the mean

standardized test—A test that uses standard procedures and scoring, with results that can be compared to a normative sample

state education agency—The state department of education

STO—Short-term objective

subjective test—A test with no specified set of answers, open for interpretation

subtest—Part of a larger test

supplemental aids and services—Aids and services that would help a student make progress in the general education classroom

TBI—Traumatic brain injury

TDD/TTY—Text telephone, or telecommunication device for the deaf

therapeutic day program—A program for students with emotional disturbance, incorporating therapy into the schedule

Title I—The federal program that provides funding for low-income schools and students

transition plan—Plan to help students get ready for postschool life

transition services—Services to help students get ready for postschool life

traumatic brain injury (TBI)—An acquired brain injury causing a functional disability

Universal Design for Learning (UDL)—A framework for designing learning environments that accommodate the widest range of abilities and needs

validity—The extent to which a test measures what it is designed to measure

visual discrimination—The ability to discern differences in color, shape, and symbols

visual-motor—Referring to the ability to coordinate vision and motor skills

vocational evaluation—Testing a student's aptitude for various areas of work

Appendix B
Definitions of Disabilities

The following definitions are taken from Section 602 of the federal Individuals with Disabilities Education Act (IDEA) of 2004 (20 U.S.C. §§ 1400 *et seq.*). The first two (*child with a disability, developmental delay*) describe broad categories of eligibility, and the remaining definitions describe specific disabilities.

child with a disability—A child evaluated [properly, who has] an intellectual impairment, a hearing impairment including deafness, a speech or language impairment, a visual impairment including blindness, serious emotional disturbance (hereafter referred to as emotional disturbance), an orthopedic impairment, autism, traumatic brain injury, another health impairment, a specific learning disability, deaf-blindness, or multiple disabilities, and who, by reason thereof, needs special education and related services.

developmental delay—The term developmental delay may be used as a disability for children aged 3 through 9, . . . and may . . . include a child (1) who is experiencing developmental delays as defined by the State and as measured by appropriate diagnostic instruments and procedures in one or more of the following areas: physical development, cognitive development, communication development, social or emotional development, or adaptive development, and (2) who, by reason thereof, needs special education and related services.

autism—A developmental disability significantly affecting verbal and non-verbal communication and social interaction, generally evident before age 3, that adversely affects a child's educational performance. Other characteristics often associated with autism are engaging in repetitive activities and stereotyped movements, resistance to environmental change or change in daily routines, and unusual responses to sensory experiences. The term does not apply if the child's educational performance is adversely affected primarily because the child has an emotional disturbance.

deaf-blindness—Concomitant hearing and visual impairments, the combination of which causes such severe communication and other developmental and educational needs that they cannot be accommodated in special education programs solely for children with deafness or children with blindness.

deafness—A hearing impairment that is so severe that the child is impaired in processing linguistic information through hearing, with or without amplification, that adversely affects a child's educational performance.

emotional disturbance—A condition exhibiting one or more of the following characteristics over a long period of time and to a marked degree that adversely affects a child's educational performance: (a) an inability to learn that cannot be explained by intellectual, sensory, or health factors; (b) an inability to build or maintain satisfactory interpersonal relationships with peers and teachers; (c) inappropriate types of behavior or feelings under normal circumstances; (d) a general pervasive mood of unhappiness or depression; (e) a tendency to develop physical symptoms or fears associated with personal or school problems. The term includes schizophrenia. The term does not apply to children who are socially maladjusted, unless it is determined that they have an emotional disturbance.

hearing impairment—An impairment in hearing, whether permanent or fluctuating, that adversely affects a child's educational performance but is not included under the definition of "deafness."

intellectual disability—Significantly subaverage general intellectual functioning, existing concurrently with deficits in adaptive behavior and manifested during the developmental period, that adversely affects a child's educational performance.

multiple disabilities—Concomitant impairments (such as intellectual disability-blindness, intellectual disability-orthopedic impairment, etc.), the combination of which causes such severe educational needs that they cannot be accommodated in a special education program solely for one of the impairments. The term does not include deaf-blindness.

orthopedic impairment—A severe orthopedic impairment that adversely affects a child's educational performance. The term includes impairments caused by congenital anomaly, impairments caused by disease (e.g., poliomyelitis, bone tuberculosis), and impairments from other causes (e.g., cerebral palsy, amputations, and fractures or burns that cause contractures).

other health impairment—Having limited strength, vitality, or alertness, including a heightened alertness to environmental stimuli, that results in limited alertness with respect to the educational environment, that (a) is due to chronic or acute health problems such as asthma, attention deficit disorder or attention deficit hyperactivity disorder, diabetes, epilepsy, a heart condition, hemophilia, lead poisoning, leukemia, nephritis, rheumatic fever, sickle cell anemia, and Tourette syndrome; and (b) adversely affects a child's educational performance.

specific learning disability—A disorder in one or more of the basic psychological processes involved in understanding or in using language, spoken or written, that may manifest itself in the imperfect ability to listen, think, speak, read, write, spell, or to do mathematical calculations. The term includes such conditions as perceptual disabilities, brain injury, minimal brain dysfunction, dyslexia, and developmental aphasia. The term does not include learning problems that are primarily the result of visual, hearing, or motor disabilities; of intellectual disability; of emotional disturbance; or of environmental, cultural, or economic disadvantage.

speech or language impairment—A communication disorder such as stuttering, impaired articulation, a language impairment, or a voice impairment that adversely affects a child's educational performance.

traumatic brain injury—An acquired injury to the brain caused by an external physical force, resulting in total or partial functional disability or psychosocial impairment, or both, that adversely affects a child's educational performance. The term applies to open or closed head injuries resulting in impairments in one or more areas, such as cognition; language; memory; attention; reasoning; abstract thinking; judgment; problem-solving; sensory, perceptual, and motor abilities; psychosocial behavior; physical functions; information processing; and speech. The term does not apply to brain injuries that are congenital or degenerative, or to brain injuries induced by birth trauma.

visual impairment, including blindness—An impairment in vision that, even with correction, adversely affects a child's educational performance. The term includes both partial sight and blindness.

Appendix C
People-First Language

People-first language is used to speak appropriately and respectfully about an individual with a disability. People-first language emphasizes the person first, not the disability. For example, when referring to a person with a disability, use phrases such as "a person who . . . ," "a person with . . . ," or "a person who has . . . ."

Here are suggestions from the Centers for Disease Control and Prevention on how to communicate with and about people with disabilities. More information is available at www.cdc.gov/disabilities.

Say . . .	Do Not Say . . .
person with a disability	disabled, handicapped
person without a disability	normal person, healthy person
person with an intellectual disability	retarded, slow, simple, moronic, defective
person with an emotional or behavioral disability	insane, crazy, psycho, maniac, nuts
person who is hard of hearing	hearing impaired, suffers a hearing loss
person who is deaf	deaf and dumb, mute
person who is blind/visually impaired	blind
person who has a communication disorder	mute, dumb

Say . . .	Do Not Say . . .
person who uses a wheelchair	confined or restricted to a wheelchair
person with a physical disability	crippled, lame, deformed, invalid, spastic
person with autism spectrum disorder	autistic
person with epilepsy or seizure disorder	epileptic
person with multiple sclerosis	afflicted by MS
person with cerebral palsy	CP victim
accessible parking or bathroom	handicapped parking or bathroom
person of short stature	midget
person with a congenital disability	birth defect
person with Down syndrome	mongoloid
person who is successful, productive	has overcome his/her disability

Appendix D
Explanations and Examples of Accommodations, Modifications, and Interventions

---

Accommodations, *modifications*, and *interventions* are terms that are often used together and interchangeably. However, as you consider the needs of students and developing an appropriate plan for them, it is imperative to understand the differences.

Accommodations are measures taken to level the playing field. They allow the student access to the general education curriculum without any changes in the content, and they do not change the task that the student is expected to do. The learning expectations and the products produced are the same for a student who is receiving accommodations as those for a student who is not.

Examples:

- Extended time for assignments
- Use of memory aids
- Frequent breaks
- Use of a multiplication table
- Preferred seating
- Tests given orally
- Reading material presented orally
- Use of a scribe

Considerations: Accommodations are used when a student is able to understand the concept but may need supports so that the disability is not interfering with performance.

Modifications are changes in the learning expectation or product, based on a learning goal that may be different than those in place for other students.

Examples:

- Reduced number or complexity of assignments
- Shortened lists of spelling words or math problems
- Use of a different grading scale

Considerations: It is important to consider what the student will have to master in order to move forward in the curriculum, whether in the current school year or in the future. Essential knowledge and skills should not be circumvented.

Interventions are instructional measures that focus on a specific academic or behavioral skill. They are used when a student needs to develop a skill that other students have already mastered. Lists of academic and behavioral interventions are available on many websites. See, for example, Intervention Central (www.interventioncentral.org) or the RTI Network (www.rtinetwork.org).

Examples:

- Interventions can include direct instruction to target a specific skill deficit (e.g., word parts, phoneme knowledge, math facts), tutoring, peer-assisted learning, behavior contracts, and menus of sensory activities.

Considerations: Interventions are intended to be intensive and very specific to a targeted skill so that the student is able to learn the skill and then be quickly moved back to the larger classroom environment.

Appendix E
Modifications by Type

Modifications of the Physical Environment
- Seat the student near the teacher.
- Seat the student where there are few distractions.
- Seat the student near a positive role model.
- Increase the distance between desks.
- Stand near the student when giving directions or presenting lessons.
- Avoid distracting stimuli (e.g., air conditioning units, high-traffic areas).
- Cover fluorescent lighting.
- Provide the student with a desk or chair that allows for movement or standing.
- Provide the student with a schedule that includes pictures or other graphics.

Modifications of Lesson Design and Delivery
- Pair students so they can check each other's work.
- Write key points on the board.
- Provide peer tutoring.
- Provide notes.
- Make sure everyone understands directions.
- Include a variety of activities during each lesson.
- Repeat directions to certain students after you have given the directions to the whole class.
- Provide a written outline.
- Allow the student to record a lesson.
- Have students review key points out loud.
- Teach via multisensory modes—visual, auditory, kinesthetic, and olfactory.
- Use computer-assisted instruction.

• Accompany oral directions with written directions (on paper or on the board) that the student can refer to as needed.

• Provide a model of the desired product, post it, and refer to it often.

• Provide cross-age peer tutoring.

• Use underlining, highlighting, and cue words to help the student find the main idea.

• Break long presentations into shorter segments.

• Eliminate information that is not critical to understanding.

Modifications to Support Organizational Skills

• Provide peer assistance.

• Assign homework buddies.

• Allow the student to have an extra set of books at home.

• Send home daily or weekly progress reports.

• Develop a reward system for in-school work and completion of homework.

• Provide a notebook for recording and completing homework assignments.

• Provide a structured routine for completing and turning in assignments.

• Teach study skills and learning strategies.

• Help the student set goals, including interim goals for long, self-paced assignments.

• Teach note-taking strategies.

• Encourage the use of color coding and highlighting for notes.

• Use visual organization strategies.

• Develop checklists for the student to use.

Modifications of Assignments/Worksheets

• Allow extra time to complete assignments and worksheets.

• Simplify or break down complex directions.

• Provide both written and oral directions.

• Distribute worksheets one at a time.

• Make sure that reading assignments are at the student's ability level.

• Require fewer correct responses; emphasize quality versus quantity.

• Shorten assignments.

• Divide work into smaller segments.

• Limit visual distractions on worksheets.

• Allow typewritten or computer-printed assignments prepared by or dictated by the student.

- Reduce the number of homework assignments.
- Do not grade down because of handwriting, spelling, or grammar.
- Do not require the use of cursive handwriting.
- Do not mark reversed or transposed letters and numbers as wrong.
- Do not require lengthy outside-reading assignments.
- Allow the student to listen to audiobooks for some reading assignments.
- Monitor the student's self-paced assignments (daily, weekly, biweekly).
- Make sure homework assignments reach home with clear, concise directions.
- Recognize and give credit for the student's oral participation in class.
- Allow the student to complete a different type of product to measure understanding.
- Provide a page number where the student can find answers.

Modifications of Testing and Testing Procedure

- Use open-book exams.
- Give exams orally.
- Give take-home tests.
- Include more objective (multiple-choice, true/false) test items and fewer items that require essay responses.
- Allow the student to type answers.
- Give frequent short quizzes instead of long exams.
- Allow extra time when testing to avoid time-related pressure on the student.
- Read test items to the student.
- Use a scribe to record the student's long answers.
- Allow for a performance task instead of a written test.
- Provide memory aids, such as use of a multiplication table.
- Provide a vocabulary key.
- Construct quizzes and tests so that answers follow the same order as the presentation of content in the material being tested.

Modifications of Behavioral Expectations

- Use timers to facilitate completion of tasks.
- Provide a structure for transitions and other unstructured times, such as during recess and assemblies, in hallways, the lunchroom, the locker room, or the library.
- Praise specific positive behaviors.
- Teach the student to use self-monitoring strategies.

• Give extra privileges and rewards for positive behavior, and do so soon after it occurs.

• Keep classroom rules simple and clear.

• Allow for short breaks between assignments.

• Use a nonverbal signal to cue the student to stay on task.

• Mark the student's correct answers, not mistakes.

• Implement a classroom behavior management system.

• Allow the student time out of seat to run errands, such as taking a note to the school office.

• Ignore inappropriate behavior that is not a serious violation of classroom rules.

• Allow legitimate movement.

• Create and enforce a behavior contract with the student.

• Involve the student by assigning tasks such as passing out and collecting papers.

• Vary activities often.

Appendix F
Checklists for Multidisciplinary Team Meetings

These checklists can help general education classroom teachers keep track of their responsibilities before, during, and after the multidisciplinary team meeting that determines whether a student should be considered to be eligible for special education services. Not every point will apply to every meeting, but all are potentially important and worth keeping in mind when discussing the eligibility of a student for special education.

Before the Meeting

As the general education classroom teacher, you should gather and review (to the best extent possible) the following documents to bring to the meeting:

- ☐ Examples of class work from the student and examples of the same assignment completed by other students for comparison
- ☐ Notes from observations of the student
- ☐ Results from screening instruments or normative tests
- ☐ Comments from previous teachers
- ☐ Copies of the student's report cards
- ☐ Comments from colleagues who work with the student (for example, the art teacher, music teacher, librarian, or physical education teacher)
- ☐ Any notes on behaviors (positive and negative) that you have kept on the student
- ☐ Summary of any interventions tried with the student
- ☐ The student's current grades
- ☐ Any accommodations or modifications currently needed for the student

During the Meeting

As the general education classroom teacher, you are likely to be one of the only education professionals in the room who has worked with the student. Others will lead the meeting, but it is very important for you to play an active role by commenting about what you know about the student's performance and interactions with others. You can contribute to the meeting in various ways.

☐ Be able to present information about the student, including the student's name, age, grade, and why you made the referral. Be able to describe in two or three sentences the difficulties the student has in the classroom, how this student compares to others, and a few of the interventions you have tried.

☐ Be prepared to describe the broader academic and social behavior of the student.

☐ Be prepared to respond to questions about the student's performance and that of others in the class.

☐ Be prepared to make a recommendation based on the information you present and the information you hear at the meeting about what type of support the student might need in order to make progress.

☐ Be willing to discuss the recommendation, working to help the team come to consensus.

☐ Weigh in on the recommendations suggested.

☐ As the others are talking and presenting their reports, take notes about how their suggestions would change instruction in the classroom for this student and for others. This is important to do regardless of whether or not the student is found eligible for special education.

After the Meeting

☐ Be available to answer any questions the parents have about the process and the report.

☐ Obtain a copy of the report and make sure it accurately reflects your assessment of the student.

☐ Read the report to gather any additional information that will help with the student in your class, or with later development of the IEP.

☐ Continue working to improve the education of the student through intervention and by talking with others. This is especially important if the student is found not to be eligible for services.

☐ If the student is found eligible, set up a meeting with the special education teacher who has the responsibility of writing the IEP. Talk with him or her about specifics, such as areas that need to be addressed in the special education program, possible goals, amount of services, times of services, and problems you have noticed.

☐ Continue gathering data on the student's progress.

References

American Speech-Language-Hearing Association (ASHA). (2015). *Questions and answers: Qualified provider provisions for related services personnel in IDEA.* Retrieved from http://www.asha.org/uploadedFiles/advocacy/federal/idea/IDEAQuestionsAnswers.pdf

Americans with Disabilities Act of 1990, 42 U.S.C. § 12101 *et seq.*

Bateman, D. F. (2005). The paperwork. In M. S. Rosenberg, D. J. O'Shea, & L. J. O'Shea (Eds.), *Student teacher to master teacher: A practical guide for educating students with special needs* (4th ed.) (pp. 209–250). Upper Saddle River, NJ: Merrill/Prentice Hall.

Board of Education of Hendrick Hudson School District v. Rowley, 458 U.S. 176, 200. (1982).

Bolt, S. (2004a). Accommodations for testing students with disabilities: Information for parents. National Association of School Psychologists. Available: http://tinyurl.com/pfcsovz

Bolt, S. (2004b). Five of the most frequently allowed accommodations in state policy: Synthesis of research. *Remedial and Special Education, 25*(3), 141–152.

Brendtro, L. K., Brokenleg, M., & Van Bockern, S. (2009). *Reclaiming our youth at risk: Our hope for the future.* Bloomington, IN: Solution Tree Media.

Brown-Chidsey, R., & Steege, M. W. (2010). *Response to Intervention: Principles and strategies for effective practice* (2nd ed.). New York: Guilford Press.

Burke, M. M. (2012). Examining family involvement in regular and special education: Lessons to be learned from both sides. *International Review of Research in Developmental Disabilities, 43*, 187–218.

Callahan, C., & Plucker, J. (2013). *Critical issues and practices in gifted education: What the research says* (2nd ed.). Washington, DC: National Association for Gifted Children.

Daniel R. R. v. State Board of Education, 874 F. 2d 1036 (5th Cir. 1989).

Davis, G. A., Rimm, S. B., & Siegle, D. (2010). *Education of the gifted and talented* (6th ed.). Upper Saddle River, NJ: Pearson.

Doe ex rel. Doe v. Bd. of Ed. of Tullahoma City Sch., 9 F.3d 455, 459-460 (6th Cir. 1993).

Family Educational Rights and Privacy Act of 1974, 20 U.S.C. § 1232g (2006).

Flexer, R. W., Baer, R. M., Luft, P., & Simmons, T. J. (2007). *Transition planning for secondary students with disabilities* (3rd ed.). Upper Saddle River, NJ: Pearson.

Friend, M., & Bursuck, W. D. (2014). *Including students with special needs: A practical guide for classroom teachers* (7th ed.). Upper Saddle River, NJ: Pearson.

Gargiulo, R. M. (2015). *Special education in contemporary society* (5th ed.). Los Angeles: Sage Publications.

Gerlach, K. (2015). *Let's team up! A checklist for teachers, paraeducators & principals.* Port Chester, NY: National Professional Resources, Inc.

Huefner, D. S., & Herr, C. M. (2012). *Navigating special education law and policy.* Verona, WI: Attainment Company.

IDEA regulations, 34 C.F.R. § 300 (2012).

Individuals with Disabilities Education Act of 2004, 20 U.S.C. § 1400 *et seq.*

Johnson, D. R., Thurlow, M., Cosia, A., & Bremer C. D. (2005). High school graduation requirements and students with disabilities. *Transition, 4* (2).

Johnson, D. R., Thurlow, M. L., & Stout, K. E. (2007). Revisiting graduation requirements and diploma options for youth with disabilities: A national study (Technical Report 49). Minneapolis, MN: University of Minnesota, National Center on Educational Outcomes. Available: http://cehd.umn.edu/NCEO/OnlinePubs/Tech49/TechReport49.pdf

Kochhar-Bryant, C. A. (with Shaw, S., & Izzo, M.). (2008). *What every teacher should know about transition and IDEA 2004.* Upper Saddle River, NJ: Pearson.

Kovaleski, J. F., VanDerHeyden, A. M., & Shapiro, E. S. (2013). *The RTI approach to evaluating learning disabilities.* New York: Guilford Press.

Letter to Cox, 110 LRP 10357. (OSEP Aug. 21, 2009).

Mastropieri, M. A., & Scruggs, T. E. (2013). *The inclusive classroom: Strategies for effective differentiated instruction* (5th ed.). Upper Saddle River, NJ: Pearson.

Morse, W. C. (1995). Comments from a biased viewpoint. In J. M. Kauffman & D. P. Hallahan (Eds.), *The illusion of full inclusion: A comprehensive critique of a current special education bandwagon* (pp. 105–120). Austin, TX: Pro-Ed.

No Child Left Behind Act. 34 CFR Part 200. (2001).

Oberti v. Board of Education of the Borough of Clementon School District, 995 F.2d 1024. (3rd Cir. 1993).

Rehabilitation Act of 1973, 29 U.S.C. § 701 *et seq.*

Roncker v. Walter, 700 F.2d 1058 (6th Cir. 1983).

Rose, D. H., Meyer, A., Strangman, N., & Rappolt, G. (2002). *Teaching every student in the digital age: Universal design for learning.* Alexandria, VA: ASCD.

Section 504 of the Rehabilitation Act of 1973, 34 C.F.R. Part 104.

Shea, T. M., & Bauer, A. M. (2011). *Behavior management: A practical approach for educators.* Upper Saddle River, NJ: Pearson.

Stipek, D. (2002). Good instruction is motivating. In A. Wigfield & J. Eccles (Eds.), *Development of achievement motivation* (pp. 309–332). San Diego: Academic Press.

Sunderman, G. L., Kim, J., S., & Orfield, G. (2005). *NCLB meets school realities: Lessons from the field.* Thousand Oaks, CA: Corwin.

U.S. Department of Education. (2012). College and career ready students. Retrieved from https://www2.ed.gov/policy/elsec/leg/blueprint/college-career-ready.pdf

U.S. Department of Education. (2013). Individuals with Disabilities Education Act: To ensure the free appropriate public education of all children with disabilities. 35th Annual Report to Congress on the Implementation of the Individuals with Disabilities Education Act. Washington, DC: Author.

U.S. Department of Education. (2015a). Improving basic programs operated by local educational agencies (Title I, Part A). Retrieved from http://www2.ed.gov/programs/titleiparta/index.html

U.S. Department of Education. (2015b). Protecting students with disabilities. Retrieved from http://www2.ed.gov/about/offices/list/ocr/504faq.html#protected

U.S. Equal Employment Opportunity Commission. (2009). Americans with Disabilities Act: Questions and answers. Retrieved from http://www.ada.gov/q&aeng02.htm

Yell, M. L. (2015). *The law and special education* (4th ed.). Upper Saddle River, NJ: Pearson.

Index

The letter *d* following a page locator denotes a definition, the letter *f* denotes a figure.

About the Authors

David F. Bateman is a professor in the Department of Educational Leadership and Special Education at Shippensburg University of Pennsylvania, where he teaches courses about learning disabilities, special education, and special education law to future teachers and administrators. Dr. Bateman has been a classroom teacher of students with learning disabilities, behavioral disorders, intellectual disabilities, and hearing impairments. A former due process hearing officer for the Commonwealth of Pennsylvania and past-president of the Pennsylvania Council for Exceptional Children, he is public policy chair of the Division for Learning Disabilities and is active in the Consortium for Citizens with Disabilities in Washington, D.C. Dr. Bateman has an MEd in special education from the College of William and Mary and a PhD in special education from the University of Kansas. Using his background as a teacher and a hearing officer, he works with school districts that have been recently involved in litigation to help them move forward successfully. He is coauthor of *The Principal's Guide to Special Education* and *The Special Education Program Administrator's Handbook*.

Jenifer L. Cline is a special education administrator in Great Falls Public Schools in Great Falls, Montana. She has an M.A. in speech language pathology from Washington State University and received her special education administrative endorsement from Montana State University Billings. Prior to earning an endorsement for special education administration, she practiced speech pathology in a variety of schools. Ms. Cline has worked as a special education administrator for the last 10 years as both the special education director of a special education cooperative and as a district-level special education administrator. She has presented on administrative topics for the American

Speech-Language-Hearing Association, the Council of Administrators of Special Education (CASE), the American Educational Research Association, and the Council for Exceptional Children (CEC). An active member of CASE and CEC, Ms. Cline has served as the president of Montana CASE and on the professional development committee for CASE. She is coauthor of *Efficient and Effective Management of Resources* and *Data: Making It Meaningful*.